INTERIOR
Rendering: Shop & Restaurant
A Practical Introduction to Architectural Illustrations

先ず，この作品集の内容に潜む現代性に注目してみたい。社会全体が多様化している中で開店するショップ
の数々。業種の増大と，様々な経営形態，加えて，意匠に求められる多国籍性や超時代感が，何の脈絡もなく
発生して，店舗デザインはどこえ行くといった感がある。そして，これを描くパースも新しい画材を駆使した
技術や表現方法が，多岐にわたって開発されている。

　パースは美術作品としての観賞と同時に，描かれた建築や店舗のデザインを解釈することができる。もとよ
り，建築を表現する目的で描かれたわけだから，パース作品集は，観点を限定した建築デザイン集でもあるわ
けだ。限定した観点というのは，パースの場合，写真とちがって，画家の感性でデザインポリシーを強調した
表現になっていることを指すのだが，時にはデザイナーの意志が正しく把握されていないこともある。その時，
デザイナーは自らの仕事に対して，思いがけない解釈のあることを知らされることになる。パース作品集は，
デザイナーとレンダラーの双方に多くの考察を呼び覚まし解答を与えてくれる。

　わが国の商店は，その在り方からして諸外国に例を見ない。地域社会そのものがヨーロッパとも，他のアジ
ア諸国とも異る独自の文化を支えてきた。過去30年間の急激な経済成長も，日本の「現代」をはかり知れない
ものとしている。

　昔の，「かさ，はきもの店」の類いは，それを必要とする人が居て商売が始められたのだが，現代では，商行為
のために需要を開発するといった方向で商店経営がなされる。定食屋の一軒があれば，独身者も食事に事欠く
ことはないのだが，各国料理にグルメブームを起して需要を拡大する消費文化の時代である。

　今日の首都圏ダウンタウンの先端をゆくショップには消費者の鼻づらをつかんで引きずりまわす程のエネル
ギーがある。経済活動としては，活発さで評価されるが，この消費文化が人に幸福な生活をもたらしているか
というと，資源の浪費と価値感の軽薄化という点で疑問が残る。

　文化は，大きな時代の流れを形成しながら常に，その一部に前衛的な部分と，伝統を固守する部分があり，
大衆は平均的時代性の中でくらしている。パース作品からショップデザインの傾向を展望すると，目を引くの

序　文

は，やはり新しいデザインの店であるが，この前衛派の示唆によって啓発される本流は，果して地に足をつけて営まれているだろうか。

　新規開店や改装工事で，都市部の商店は絶えず新陳代謝している。しかし，大きな動きというものは決して性急ではない。うつり変わる流行をやり過ごしながらもそれらを平均的にとらえてゆっくりしたテンポで変身してゆく。この本流がパース作品で見ても今ひとつ安堵させるものが見当らない。多様化への過渡期で目標を見失っているとするのが好意的解釈だ。新らしさへの憧れが，かえって流行に染まって没個性を招くというジレンマが見られる。眞物を追求しなくては新らしいものを生み出すことはできないという大原則が忘れられているのだ。

　「しっとりとした佇まい」という言葉のあてはまるショップがあるとしたら，逆説的だが，それが個性の発露だといえよう。

　安定経済への道を歩むこれからの日本では，熟成された佳き建築が望まれもし，つくられるにちがいない。

　レンダラーの中にはデザインワークもこなす人があるが，どちらかと言えば，レンダラーは評論家の立場であろう。作画を通じて多くのデザインに接し，それらを解釈する習慣が観賞眼をも養うことになる。

　但し，店舗の内装工事については，デザイナーの描いたパースがプレゼンテーションに用いられ，時には宣伝物にまで用いられるケースも少くない。言い替えればパースの描けるデザイナーが存在するということである。この人達に期待するところは大きい。なぜなら実務の中で施主に対する強い説得力を持つことになるから，時代の舵をもとり得る立場にあるのだ。

　本書に集録した作品の中にもデザイナーの手によるものがあって，設計意図がストレートに表現されているのだが，パースを見ただけでは他と区別することはできない。

　ともあれ，豊かな資材と情報のあふれる今は，ショップ＆レストランづくりに携わる人達がそれぞれの立場で仕事を昇華して，心も豊かな店々が利用できる日を待とう。

Preface

Initially I would like to take a look at the hidden modernity of the works in this collection. There are many shops that continue to operate in a society that is entirely versified. With the originality of multi-internationality and the extra trendiness borne with the times that is demanded for design, in addition to the increase in types of industries and various forms of management that appear to follow no singular thread, the direction of shop design seems to be unclear. Accordingly, the techniques and expressive methods indicated within these drawings make good use of the latest painting materials and have been developed in various ranges.

A perspective drawing offers a commentry on the architectural plan and shop design, and at the same time serves as an appreciative work of art in itself. Owing to the fact that a perspective drawing is created in order to express the work of the architect, a collection of such drawings may be looked upon as a compilation of architectural art of which the point of view is limited. This means that the policy of design is emphasized in accordance to the sense of the artist unlike the end product of a photograph. This could sometimes lead to the will of the designer being mis-translated in the actual drawing. Such cases will shock the designers into realizing that there are other ways to interpret their work. This collection of work will therefore act as a reminder to both designers and readers that solutions may be found by viewing the work from different angles.

The style of shops in Japan may be expected to be totally different from those of other countries. We have managed to maintain a cultural independence of other communities in European and Asian countries. In addition to this, the rapid development of the Japanese economy over the past thirty years has made the present era incalculable.

Retail outlets such as umbrella shops or clog shops were able to go into business owing to the fact that there was a public that needed their wares. Nowadays, however, such shops can only exist by carefully studying the laws of supply and demand. Although a single restaurant with a mixed menu is enough to prevent the starvation of several bachelors, it is now the age where this restaurant has to recognize the fact that supply and demand is ready to create a boom in international gourment dishes.

The leading downtown shops of today's metropolis have enough energy to pull their customers around by their noses. From the aspect of economics this is a good thing, but one cannot help but wonder if this consumer-orientated society is in fact bringing us the good life we have come to expect when we concentrate on the mineral waste and lack of sincerity that out sense of valuse are being bombarded with.

In order to flow with the current of modern times, it is necessary to recognize that culture is split into two distinct categories ; one that is avant-gard, and the other that strives to maintain traditional customs. Most people of today's age exist within a well-balanced vacuum. Glancing thourgh the trends in perspective drawings, ones attention is naturally drawn to this shops that utilize new designs. However, I must admit to sometimes wondering if the suggestive power of this group of avant-gard artists is really running with its feet its feet on the ground.

With new establishment and refurbishments, the shops in the cities are constantly being replaced. However, this replacement is not overly hasty which brings about the effect that the transformations are in keeping with the pace of fashion. The trends of perspective drawing still leave something to be desired in order to stay in the main stream. To put it politely, it is losing its original aim by occuring in mid-period when the market is flooded with diversification. A yearning for newness only acts to put people in a dilemma that will eventually bring about a loss of personality which results from having been deeply steeped in fashion. The main principle which states that the creation of new art-forms is impossible without the carefull studying of their original forms is totally forgotten here.

To say that a shop has a "quiet appearence" could in fact be a paradoxical expression of personality.

In Japan's future, where the stability of the economy has been ensured, carefully planned houses will surely come into demand and will be constructed.

Some perspective artists are also capable of design, but I really feel that they should stay in their original duty as critics. The frequent contact that they get from various designs and the practice of interpreting them gives them the perfect opportunity of improving their powers of appreciation.

There are many cases where perspective drawings created by the designers are used as presentations or as publication materials for the finished products of interior shop design. In other words, there are some designers who are also able to produce perspective drawings.

We may place a great deal of expectation on these people as they have a stroong influence over their benefactors. They are in the position to control the trends of the times.

Contained within these cover is a collection of the work produced by these designers. The intention of the plan is expressed straightforwardly, but it is difficult to tell the difference between each merely by looking at the perspective drawings.

We have now reached an age which is wealthy in materials and information, and we can but hope that the day will come when the people who control the outlook of shops and restaurants will sublimate their duties in accordance to their individual positions to make a gender of generous-minded shopkeepers who are easy to work with.

『ガッシュとエアブラシの混合描法』進士竜一
"The Combined Drawing Method of Gouache and Airbrush" by Ryuichi Shinji

目　次
C O N T E N T S

凡例 (データの読み方)

a: 建築物名称

b: 所在地

c: 設計事務所

d: パース作画者

e: 出品者

LEGEND (A Guide to How to Read Data)

a: Project Title

b: Location

c: Planning Office

d: Renderer

e: Applicant

INTERIOR RENDERING : SHOP & RESTAURANT

Edited by Graphic-sha Editorial Staff

Copyright © 1990 by Graphic-sha Publishing Co., Ltd.

This revised edition was published in 1994 by
Graphic-sha Publishing Co., Ltd.
1-9-12 Kudan-kita Chiyoda-ku Tokyo 102 Japan
Phone : 81 3 3263 4318 Fax : 81 3 3263 5297

ISBN4-7661-0546-X

Printed in Hong Kong by Everbest Printing Co., Ltd.

1.飲食専門店

1.Eating and Drinking

西洋料理
日本料理
各種高級レストラン
ファミリー・レストラン
カフェ・レストラン
バー
クラブ
スナック
ファースト・フード
喫茶店……他

Western food
Japanese food
Various Hight-class Restaurants
Family Restaurant
Café Restaurant
Bar
Club
Snack Bar
Fastfood Restaurant
Coffee Shop……etc.

a: 六本木V
b: 東京都港区六本木
c: C.D.W.ジパング
d: 柳川敏行
e: 柳川敏行
●
a: ROPPONGI-V PLAN
b: Roppongi, Minato-ku, Tokyo
c: C.D.W.JIPANG
d: Toshiyuki Yanagawa
e: Toshiyuki Yanagawa

a: Pレストラン
b: 東京都港区
d: 高野浩毅
e: インテリア・ライフ101/高野浩毅

a: P RESTAURANT PLAN
b: Minato-ku, Tokyo
d: Hiroki Takano
e: Interior Life 101/Hiroki Takano

a: Iレストラン
b: 大阪府大阪市
c: 総合店舗センター
d: 高野浩毅
e: インテリア・ライフ101/高野浩毅

a: I RESTAURANT
b: Osaka-shi, Osaka
c: Sogo Tenpo Senter
d: Hiroki Takano
e: Interior Life 101/Hiroki Takano

a: SEA & RESTAURANT VIVO
b: 香川県高松市
c: 三木建築設計事務所/三木雅愛
d: 金本正
e: 金本正
●
a: SEA & RESTAURANT VIVO
b: Takamatsu-shi, Kagawa Pref.
c: Miki Architect Design Office/Masachika Miki
d: Tadashi Kanemoto
e: Tadashi Kanemoto

a: セルダムシーン飲食店
b: 宮城県蔵王町
c: 株式会社潤建築工房
d: 庄司澄子
e: 庄司澄子
●
a: SELDOM SCENE RESTAURANT PLAN
b: Zao-cho, Miyagi Pref.
c: JUN Architectural Design Office
d: Sumiko Shoji
e: Sumiko Shoji

a: セルダムシーン飲食店
b: 宮城県蔵王町
c: 株式会社潤建築工房
d: 庄司澄子
e: 庄司澄子
●
a: SELDOM SCENE RESTAURANT PLAN
b: Zao-cho, Miyagi Pref.

a: カジュアルレストラン チャヤ
b: 宮城県大河原町
c: 株式会社潤建築工房
d: 庄司澄子
e: 庄司澄子
●
a: CASUAL RESTAURANT CHAYA
b: Ogawara-machi, Miyagi Pref.
c: JUN Architectural Design Office
d: Sumiko Shoji
e: Sumiko Shoji

a: 千代田カントリー倶楽部メンバーズレストラン
b: 茨城県
c: まなべみどりインテリアデザイン事務所
d: 海法一夫
e: 海法一夫

a: CHIYODA COUNTRY CLUB-MEMBER'S RESTAURANT
b: Ibaragi Pref.
c: Manabe Midori Interior Design Co., Ltd.
d: Itsuo Kaiho
e: Itsuo Kaiho

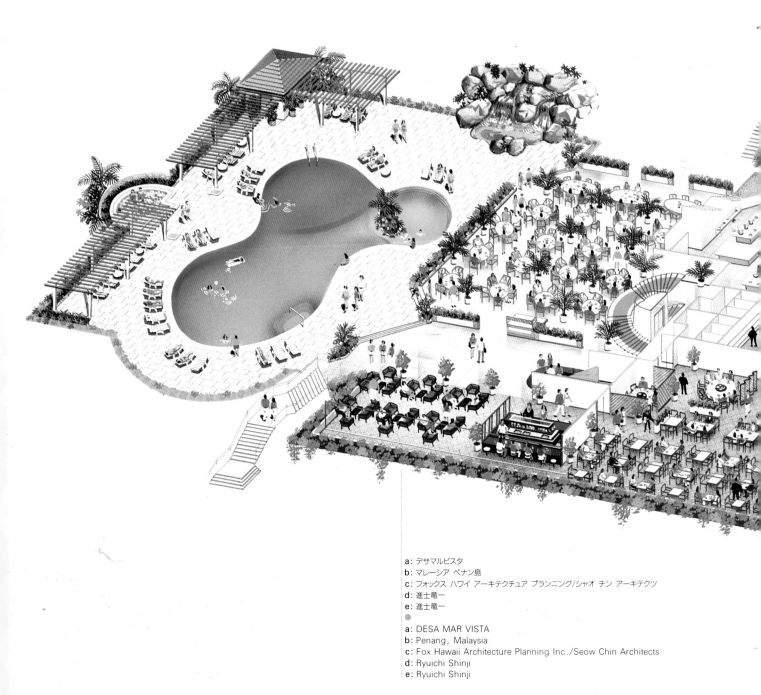

a: デサマルビスタ
b: マレーシア ペナン島
c: フォックス ハワイ アーキテクチュア プランニング/シャオ チン アーキテクツ
d: 進士竜一
e: 進士竜一

●
a: DESA MAR VISTA
b: Penang, Malaysia
c: Fox Hawaii Architecture Planning Inc./Seow Chin Architects
d: Ryuichi Shinji
e: Ryuichi Shinji

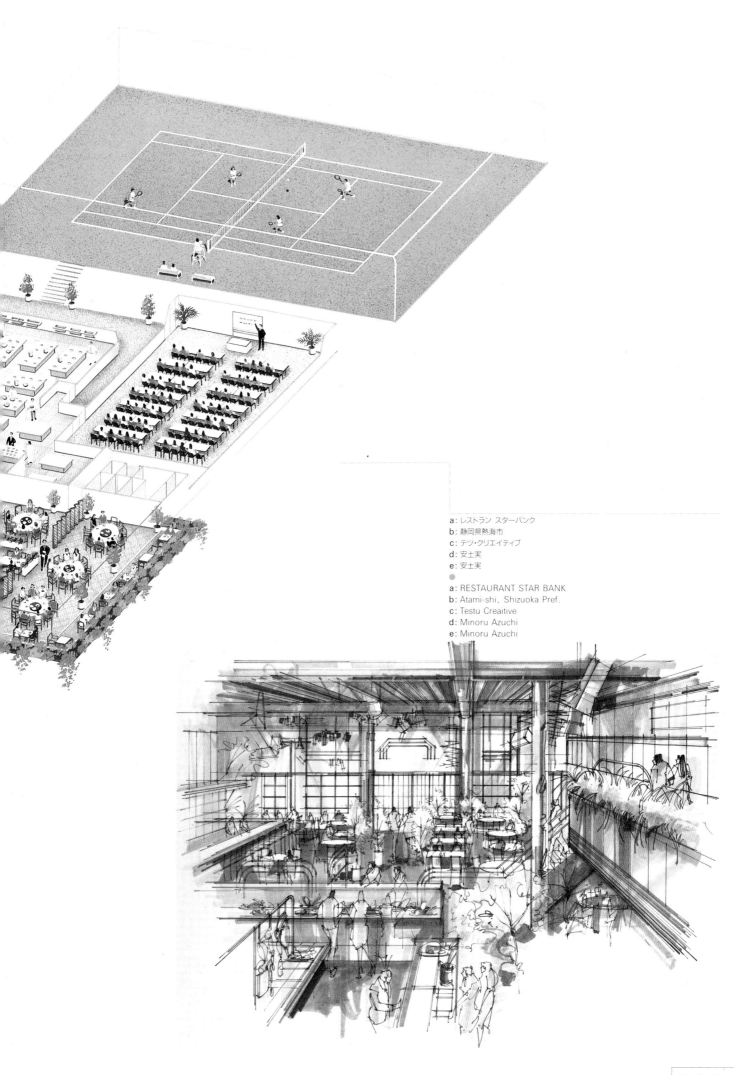

a: レストラン スターバンク
b: 静岡県熱海市
c: テツ・クリエイティブ
d: 安土実
e: 安土実

a: RESTAURANT STAR BANK
b: Atami-shi, Shizuoka Pref.
c: Testu Creaitive
d: Minoru Azuchi
e: Minoru Azuchi

a: ホテル内レストラン
b: 京都府
c: スペースデザイン・オブジェ
d: 沢崎達彦
e: 株式会社コラム・デザインセンター

a: HOTEL-RESTAURANT
b: Kyoto
c: Space Design Objet
d: Tatsuhiko Sawazaki
e: Column Design Center Inc.

a: レストラン
c: ミア・インテリア・アソシエイト
d: 仲田貴代史
e: 株式会社コラム・デザインセンター

a: RESTAURANT
c: Mia Interior Associate
d: Kiyoshi Nakata
e: Column Design Center Inc.

a: ふれあいステーキコーナー
b: 東京都
c: スペースデザイン・オブジェ
d: 矢野哲也
e: 株式会社コラム・デザインセンター

a: FUREAI STEAK CORNER
b: Tokyo
c: Space Design Objet
d: Tetsuya Yano
e: Column Design Center Inc.

a: レストラン
d: 仲田貴代史
e: 株式会社コラム・デザインセンター

a: RESTAURANT
d: Kiyoshi Nakata
e: Column Design Center Inc.

a: 西川屋
b: 愛知県名古屋市
c: カトウ美装株式会社
d: 譚少芝
e: 譚少芝

a: NISHIKAWAYA
b: Nagoya-shi, Aichi Pref.
c: Kato Biso Co., Ltd.
d: Tan Shao Zhi
e: Tan Shao Zhi

a: 好水
b: 神奈川県小田原市
c: 門松廣司建築研究所/インテリア・ライフ101
d: 高野浩毅
e: インテリア・ライフ101/高野浩毅

a: YOSHIMIZU
b: Odawara-shi, Kanagawa Pref.
c: Kadomatu Architects Office/Interior Life 101
d: Hiroki Takano
e: Interior Life 101/Hiroki Takano

a: 伏虎園
b: 和歌山県和歌山市
c: アスカ企画
d: 建築パース・アトリエ・ノバ/吉村勲
e: 建築パース・アトリエ・ノバ/吉村勲
●
a: FUKKOEN
b: Wakayama-shi, Wakayama Pref.
c: Asuka Kikaku
d: Kenchiku Pers Atelier NOVA/Isao Yoshimura
e: Kenchiku Pers Atelier NOVA/Isao Yoshimura

a: ヒルトップ松城
b: 静岡県浜松市
c: 須山建設株式会社
d: 和田宅矛
e: 造研
●
a: HILL TOP MATSUSHIRO
b: Hamamatsu-shi, Shizuoka Pref.
c: Suyama Kensetsu Co., Ltd
d: Takumu Wada
e: Zoken

a: 玄界灘
b: 静岡県浜松市
c: 株式会社大木建築設計事務所
d: 和田宅矛
e: 造研

a: GENKAINADA
b: Hamamatsu-shi, Shizuoka Pref.
c: Oki Architectural Planning Office
d: Takumu Wada
e: Zoken

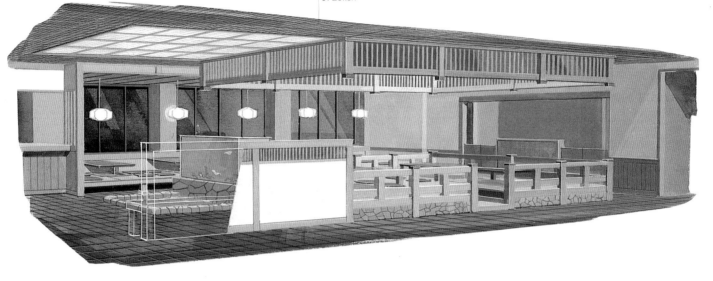

a: スシバー レッドポギー
b: 北海道札幌市
c: 和田裕設計室
d: 安土実
e: 安土実

a: SUSHI BAR RED PORGY
b: Sapporo-shi, Hokkaido
c: Wada Degin Studio
d: Minoru Azuchi
e: Minoru Azuchi

a: 活魚料理海彦山彦
b: 宮城県仙台市
c: 株式会社潤建築工房
d: 庄司澄子
e: 庄司澄子
●
a: SEAFOODS RESTAURANT-UMIHIKO YAMAHIKO
b: Sendai-shi, Miyagi Pref.
c: JUN Architectural Design Office
d: Sumiko Shoji
e: Sumiko Shoji

a: うなぎ串焼の店
b: 東京都港区
c: JANインテリア設計事務所
d: 高野浩毅
e: インテリア・ライフ101/高野浩毅
●
a: JAPANESE RESTAURANT
b: Minato-ku, Tokyo
c: JAN Interior Office
d: Hiroki Takano
e: Interior Life 101/Hiroki Takano

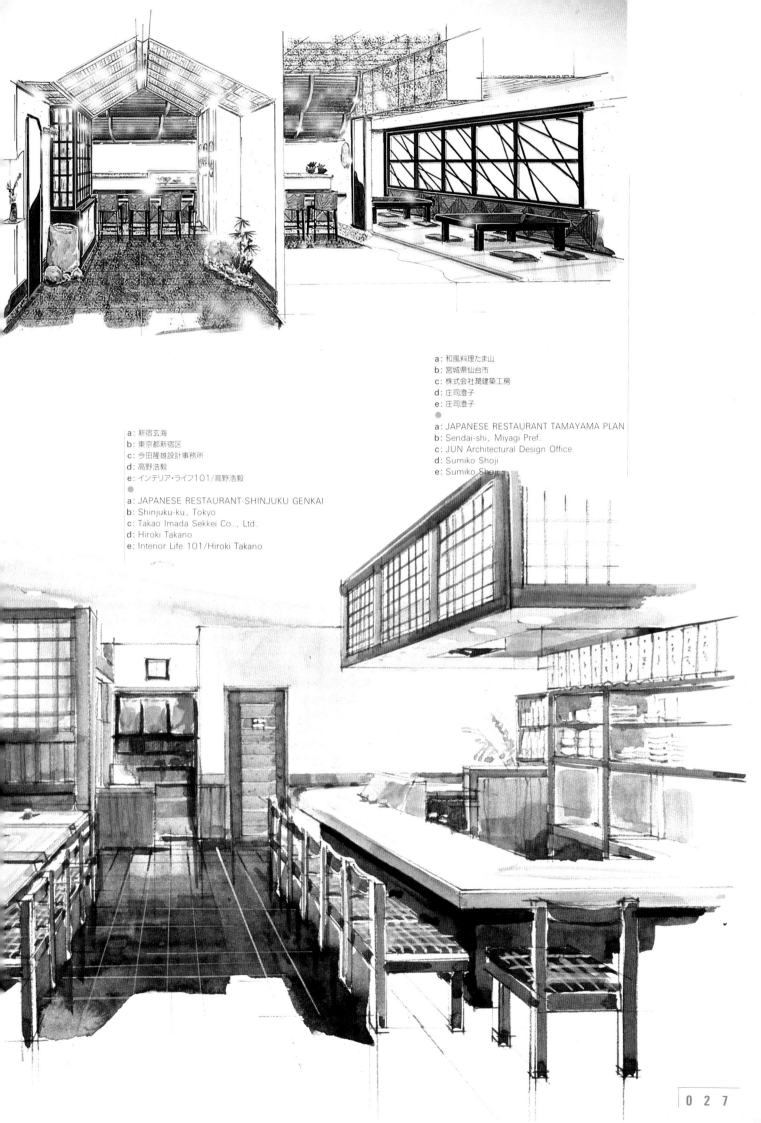

a: 和風料理たま山
b: 宮城県仙台市
c: 株式会社潤建築工房
d: 庄司澄子
e: 庄司澄子

a: JAPANESE RESTAURANT TAMAYAMA PLAN
b: Sendai-shi, Miyagi Pref.
c: JUN Architectural Design Office
d: Sumiko Shoji
e: Sumiko Shoji

a: 新宿玄海
b: 東京都新宿区
c: 今田隆雄設計事務所
d: 高野浩毅
e: インテリア・ライフ101/高野浩毅

a: JAPANESE RESTAURANT-SHINJUKU GENKAI
b: Shinjuku-ku, Tokyo
c: Takao Imada Sekkei Co., Ltd.
d: Hiroki Takano
e: Interior Life 101/Hiroki Takano

a: うどん店
c: 西原由人デザインオフィス
d: 川嶋俊介
e: 川嶋俊介

a: UDON SHOP
c: Yoshito Nishihara Design Office
d: Shunsuke Kawashima
e: Shunsuke Kawashima

a: 中華レストラン天馬
b: 兵庫県芦屋市
c: 株式会社高島屋
d: 井内一夫
e: 井内一夫
●
a: CHINESE RESTAURANT TENMA
b: Ashiya-shi, Hyogo Pref.
c: Takashimaya Co., Ltd.
d: Kazuo Inouchi
e: Kazuo Inouchi

a: 自然食レストラン彩
b: グァム
c: アヅチ・プランニングスタジオ
d: 安土実
e: 安土実
●
a: NATURAL FOODS
   RESTAURANT SAI
b: Guam
c: Azuchi Planning Studio
d: Minoru Azuchi
e: Minoru Azuchi

a: エスニックレストラン
d: 仲田貴代史
e: 株式会社コラム・デザインセンター 〉
●
a: ETHNIC RESTAURANT
d: Kiyoshi Nakata
e: Column Design Center Inc.

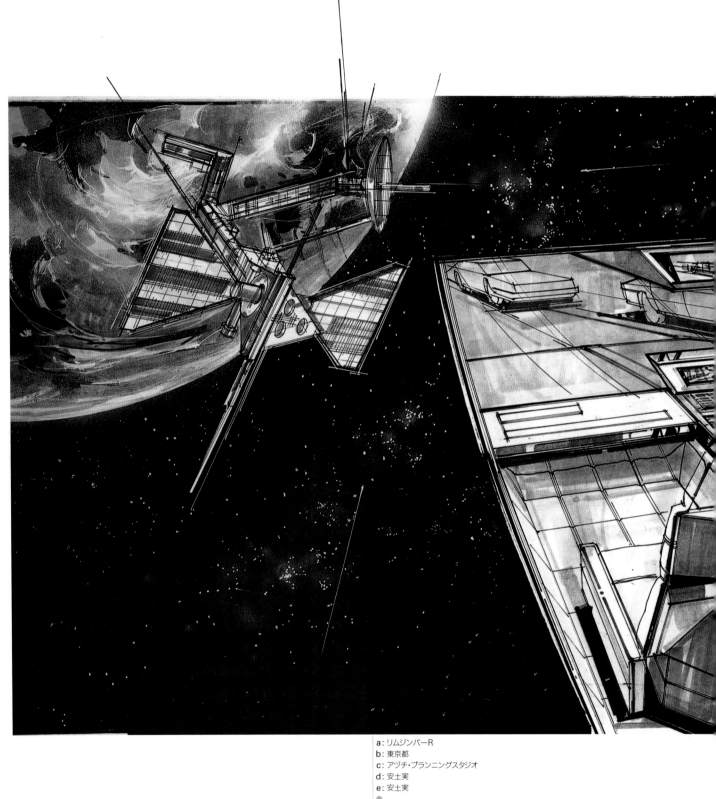

a: リムジンバーR
b: 東京都
c: アヅチ・プランニングスタジオ
d: 安土実
e: 安土実

a: LIMOUSINE BAR R
b: Tokyo
c: Azuchi Planning Studio
d: Minoru Azuchi
e: Minoru Azuchi

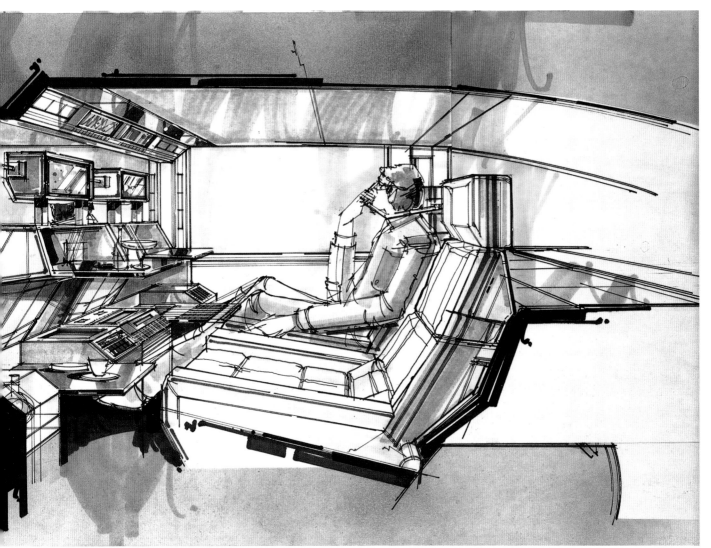

a: リムジンバーR
b: 東京都
c: アヅチ・プランニングスタジオ
d: 安土実
e: 安土実

a: LIMUOSINE BAR R
b: Tokyo
c: Azuchi Planning Studio
d: Minoru Azuchi
e: Minoru Azuchi

a: クレプシドラ   a: CLEPSYDRA
c: 進士竜一   c: Ryuichi Shinji
d: 進士竜一   d: Ryuichi Shinji
e: 進士竜一   e: Ryuichi Shinji

a: 会員制クラブA   a: MEMBER, S CLUB A
b: 新潟県新潟市   b: Niigata-shi, Niigata Pref.
c: 株式会社童夢住   c: Doms Co., Ltd.
d: 長谷川久彦   d: Hisahiko Hasegawa
e: 長谷川久彦   e: Hisahiko Hasegawa

a: マンボウズ　　　　　　　　　　a: MANBOW'S
b: 静岡県清水市　　　　　　　　　b: Shimizu-shi, Shizuoka Pref.
c: 株式会社造型資源開発研究所　　c: JETE
d: 加藤春枝　　　　　　　　　　　d: Harue Kato
e: ケイズ　　　　　　　　　　　　e: Keiz

a: カフェバー ビュー　　　　　　a: CAFE BAR VIEW
b: 神奈川県横浜市　　　　　　　　b: Yokohama-shi, Kanagawa Pref.
c: アヅチ・プランニングスタジオ　c: Azuchi Planning Studio
d: 安土実　　　　　　　　　　　　d: Minoru Azuchi
e: 安土実　　　　　　　　　　　　e: Minoru Azuchi

a: グリーンフィールド
b: 大阪府大阪市
c: 石橋清志建築設計事務所
d: 川原崎由夫
e: 川原崎由夫
●
a: GREEN FIELD
b: Osaka-shi, Osaka
c: Ishibashi Kiyoshi Architectural Drafting Office
d: Yoshio Kawarasaki
e: Yoshio Kawarasaki

a: 居酒屋
b: 大阪府大阪市新大阪駅内
c: 株式会社アイ・ディ・エス企画
d: 笠原征人
e: 笠原征人

●
a: IZAKAYA (TAVERN)
b: Shin-Osaka Station, Osaka-shi, Osaka
c: I.D.S.Planning Co., Ltd.
d: Masato Kasahara
e: Masato Kasahara

a: レストラン・ディスコ・バー クロスポイント
b: 神奈川県横浜市
c: 和田裕設計室
d: 安土実
e: 安土実

a: RESTAURANT DISCO BAR X'POINT
b: Yokohama-shi, Kanagawa Pref.
c: Wada Desin Studio
d: Minoru Azuchi
e: Minoru Azuchi

a: スナックA
b: 宮城県仙台市
c: 株式会社潤建築工房
d: 庄司澄子
e: 庄司澄子

a: SNACK BAR A PLAN
b: Sendai-shi, Miyagi Pref.
c: JUN Architectural Design Office
d: Sumiko Shoji
e: Sumiko Shoji

a: スナックB
b: 宮城県大河原町
c: 株式会社潤建築工房
d: 庄司澄子
e: 庄司澄子

a: SNACK BAR B PLAN
b: Ogawara-machi, Miyagi Pref.
c: JUN Architectural Design Office
d: Sumiko Shoji
e: Sumiko Shoji

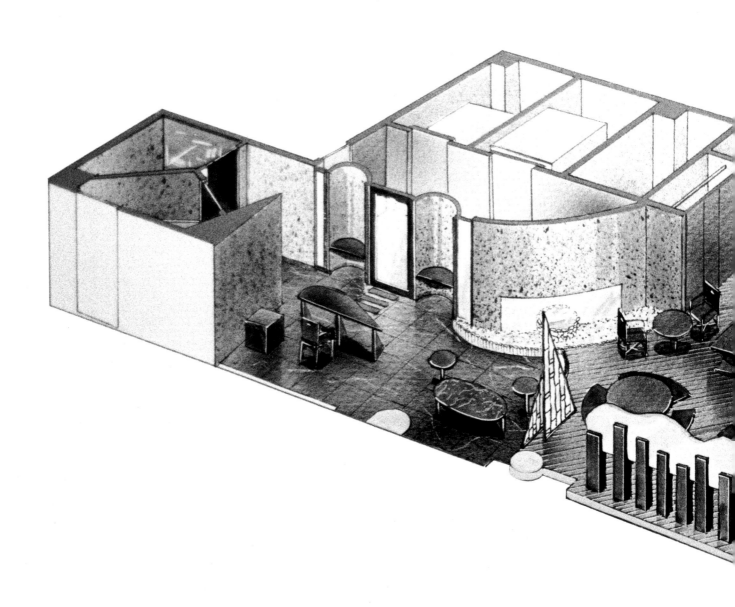

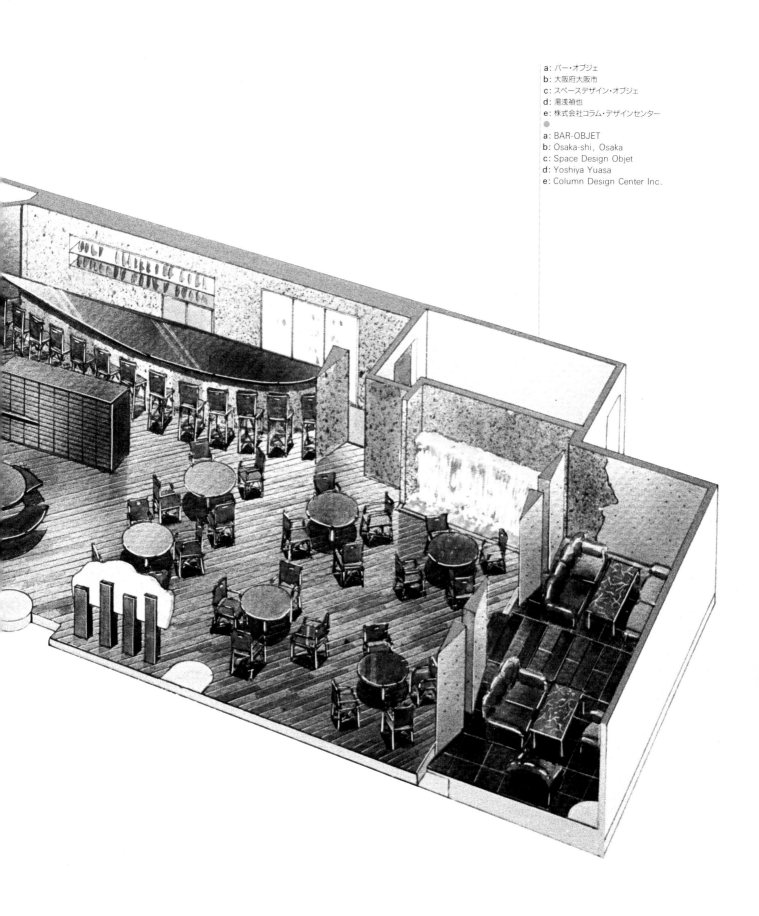

a: バー・オブジェ
b: 大阪府大阪市
c: スペースデザイン・オブジェ
d: 湯浅禎也
e: 株式会社コラム・デザインセンター

a: BAR-OBJET
b: Osaka-shi, Osaka
c: Space Design Objet
d: Yoshiya Yuasa
e: Column Design Center Inc.

a: スナックC
b: 宮城県大河原町
c: 株式会社潤建築工房
d: 庄司澄子
e: 庄司澄子

a: SNACK BAR C PLAN
b: Ogawara-machi, Miyagi Pref.
c: JUN Architectural Design Office
d: Sumiko Shoji
e: Sumiko Shoji

a: ラウンジ アクア・マリーン
b: 愛知県名古屋市
c: 株式会社山田デザイン事務所
d: 株式会社山田デザイン事務所/山田久仁夫
e: 株式会社山田デザイン事務所/山田久仁夫

a: LOUNGE-AQUA MARINE
b: Nagoya-shi, Aichi Pref.
c: Yamada Design Office Co.
d: Yamada Design Office Co./Kunio Yamada
e: Yamada Design Office Co./Kunio Yamada

a: クラブドゥー
b: 和歌山県和歌山市
c: アスカ企画/DOM設計
d: 建築パース・アトリエ・ノバ/吉村勲
e: 建築パース・アトリエ・ノバ/吉村勲

a: CLUB DEUX
b: Wakayama-shi, Wakayama Pref.
c: Asuka Kikaku/DOM Sekkei
d: Kenchiku Pers Atelier NOVA/Isao Yoshimura
e: Kenchiku Pers Atelier NOVA/Isao Yoshimura

a: ジャジャクラブ
b: 愛知県名古屋市
c: 株式会社エム・ディー
d: 加藤春枝
e: ケイズ

a: JA-JA CLUB
b: Nagoya-shi, Aichi Pref.
c: MD Co.
d: Harue Kato
e: Keiz

a：スナック
b：兵庫県姫路市
c：株式会社不二商
d：隼デザイン事務所/四海隼一
e：四海隼一

a: SNACK BAR
b: Himeji-shi, Hyogo Pref.
c: Fuji-sho Ltd.
d: Hayabusa Design Office/Shunichi Shikai
e: Shunichi Shikai

a: パブレストラン マッシーの店
b: 新潟県新潟市
c: 佐々木設計
d: 長谷川久彦
e: 長谷川久彦

a: PUB RESTAURANT-MASSE
b: Niigata-shi, Niigata Pref.
c: Sasaki Architectural Office
d: Hisahiko Hasegawa
e: Hisahiko Hasegawa

a: カフェ・レスト FUKKOEN
b: 和歌山県和歌山市
c: アスカ企画
d: 建築パース・アトリエ・ノバ/吉村勲
e: 建築パース・アトリエ・ノバ/吉村勲
●
a: CAFE RESTAURANT-FUKKOEN
b: Wakayama-shi, Wakayama Pref.
c: Asuka Kikaku
d: Kenchiku Pers Atelier NOVA/Isao Yoshimura
e: Kenchiku Pers Atelier NOVA/Isao Yoshimura

a: お好み焼&喫茶店
c: ミア・インテリア・アソシエイト
d: 仲田貴代史
e: 株式会社コラム・デザインセンター

a: OKONOMI-YAKI & TEAROOM
c: Mia Interior Associate
d: Kiyoshi Nakata
e: Column Design Center Inc.

a: ファーストフーズレストラン
b: 宮城県仙台市
c: 株式会社潤建築工房
d: 庄司澄子
e: 庄司澄子

a: FAST FOODS RESTAURANT PLAN
b: Sendai-shi, Miyagi Pref.
c: JUN Architectural Design Office
d: Sumiko Shoji
e: Sumiko Shoji

a: サンドイッチハウス エントランスホール　　a: SANDWICH HOUSE PLAN-ENTRANCE HALL
b: 静岡県　　　　　　　　　　　　　　　　　b: Shizuoka Pref.
c: 株式会社イセキ　　　　　　　　　　　　　c: Iseki Co., Ltd.
d: 譚少芝　　　　　　　　　　　　　　　　　d: Tan Shao Zhi
e: 譚少芝　　　　　　　　　　　　　　　　　e: Tan Shao Zhi

a: サンドイッチハウス 客席ホール　　a: SANDWICH HOUSE PLAN-GUEST HALL
b: 静岡県　　　　　　　　　　　　　b: Shizuoka Pref.
c: 株式会社イセキ　　　　　　　　　c: Iseki Co., Ltd.
d: 譚少芝　　　　　　　　　　　　　d: Tan Shao Zhi
e: 譚少芝　　　　　　　　　　　　　e: Tan Shao Zhi

a: FROG2階
b: 愛知県名古屋市
c: カトウ美装株式会社
d: 譚少芝
e: 譚少芝

a: FROG PLAN 2F
b: Nagoya-shi, Aichi Pref.
c: Kato Biso CO., LTD.
d: Tan Shao Zhi
e: Tan Shao Zhi

a: FROG1階
b: 愛知県名古屋市
c: カトウ美装株式会社
d: 譚少芝
e: 譚少芝

a: FROG PLAN 1F
b: Nagoya-shi, Aichi Pref.
c: Kato Biso Co., Ltd.
d: Tan Shao Zhi
e: Tan Shao Zhi

a: バンチューラ
b: 東京都中央区日本橋
c: 株式会社石橋徳川建築設計所
d: 大山記糸夫
e: 株式会社Room T/高橋弘
●
a: PANCHELA
b: Nihonbashi, Chuo-ku, Tokyo
c: Ishibashi, Tokugawa & Associates, Architects
d: Kishio Oyama
e: Room T Co., Ltd./Hiroshi Takahashi

a: 京急クアリゾート平和島
b: 東京都大田区
c: 西松建設株式会社
d: 小野垣晋一
e: 有限会社ヒューマン・ファクター

a: HEIWAJIMA KUR HOUSE
b: Ota-ku, Tokyo
c: Nishimatsu Kensetsu Co., Ltd.
d: Shinichi Onogaki
e: Human Factor Ltd.

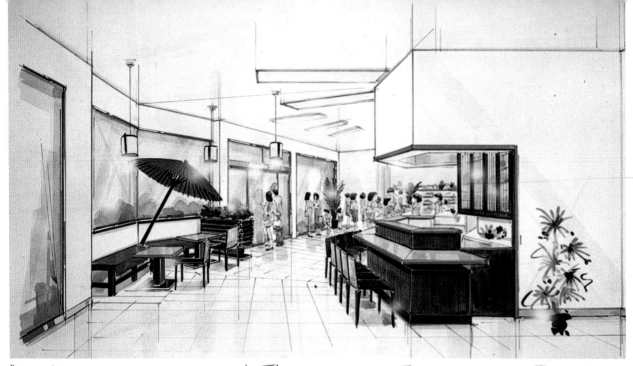

a: レストランバー フィニー
b: ロスアンゼルス
c: コンセプトキュー
d: 安土実
e: 安土実

a: RESTAURANT & BAR FINI
b: Losangels
c: Concept Kyu
d: Minoru Azuchi
e: Minoru Azuchi

a: 南茶屋
b: 宮城県名取市
c: 株式会社潤建築工房
d: 庄司澄子
e: 庄司澄子

a: CAFE & SNACK MINAMI CHA-YA
b: Natori-shi, Miyagi Pref.
c: JUN Architectural Design Office
d: Sumiko Shoji
e: Sumiko Shoji

a: カフェ蔵シック
b: 宮城県原町
c: 株式会社潤建築工房
d: 庄司澄子
e: 庄司澄子

a: CAFE CLASSICC
b: Haranomachi, Miyagi Pref.
c: JUN Architectural Design Office
d: Sumiko Shoji
e: Sumiko Shoji

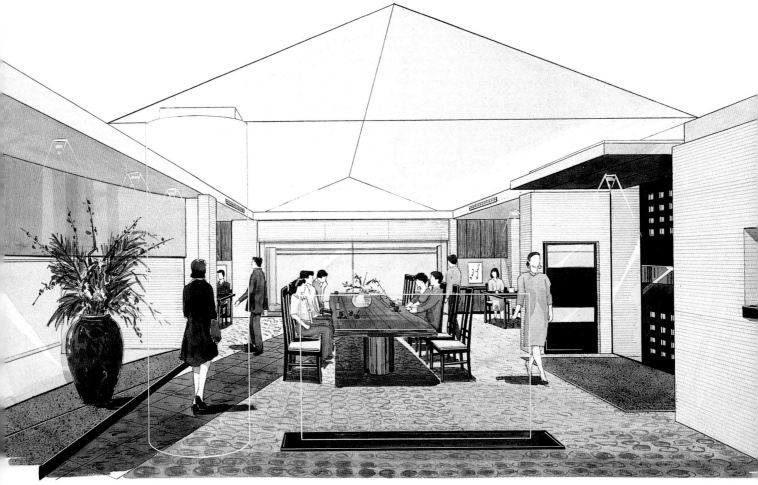

a: 喫茶「路」
b: 京都府京都市左京区
c: 株式会社イシダ建築デザイン・設計部
d: 株式会社イシダ建築デザイン/坂根元
e: 株式会社イシダ建築デザイン・デザイン部

●
a: TEAROOM MICHI
b: Sakyo-ku, Kyoto-shi, Kyoto
c: Ishida Architectural Design Office Co., Planning Section
d: Ishida Architectural Design Office Co./Hajime Sakane
e: Ishida Architectural Design Office Co., Design Section

a: 茶屋亭京橋店
b: 大阪府大阪市
c: 株式会社コラム・デザインセンター
d: 宮後浩
e: 株式会社コラム・デザインセンター

a: RESTAURANT CHAYATEI-KYOBASHI BRANCHI
b: Osaka-shi, Osaka
c: Column Design Center Inc.
d: Hiroshi Miyago
e: Column Design Center Inc.

a: ネオイタリアンカフェ・スタジオーニ
b: 群馬県高崎市
c: デザインルーム・サイトウ
d: とみあとりえ/斉藤富子
e: とみあとりえ/斉藤富子

a: NEO ITALIAN CAFE-SUTADIONI
b: Takasaki-shi, Gunma Pref.
c: Design Room Saito
d: Tomi Atelier/Tomiko Saito
e: Tomi Atelier/Tomiko Saito

a: ビル内コーヒーラウンジ
b: 千葉県
d: 宮後浩
e: 株式会社コラム・デザインセンター

a: COFFEE LOUNGE
b: Chiba Pref.
d: Hiroshi Miyago
e: Column Design Center Inc.

a: リフレッシュメントルーム
b: 東京都
c: 株式会社松坂製作所
d: 小倉通子
e: 小倉通子

●

a: REFRESHMENT ROOM
b: Tokyo
c: Matsuzaka Seisakujo Co., Ltd.
d: Michiko Ogura
e: Michiko Ogura

a: 茶衣華　　　　　　.a: CHAIHANA
b: 新潟県新潟市　　　 b: Niigata-shi, Niigata Pref.
c: 越後観光株式会社　 c: Echigo Kanko Co., Ltd.
d: 長谷川久彦　　　　 d: Hisahiko Hasegawa
e: 長谷川久彦　　　　 e: Hisahiko Hasegawa

a: コンフォート大手前
b: 大阪府大阪市
c: 大成建設
d: 村山善次郎
e: 村山善次郎

a: COMFORT OTEMAE
b: Osaka-shi, Osaka
c: Taisei Corporation
d: Zenjiro Murayama
e: Zenjiro Murayama

FRONT

a: 富山第一ホテル コーヒーハウス
b: 富山県
c: 株式会社日本設計事務所
d: 近藤喬枝
e: 近藤喬枝

a: TOYAMA DAIICHI HOTEL-TEA LOUNG
b: Toyama Pref.
c: Nihon Sekkei Office Co., Ltd.
d: Takae Kondo
e: Takae Kondo

a: 富山第一ホテル バー
b: 富山県
c: 株式会社日本設計事務所
d: 近藤喬枝
e: 近藤喬枝

a: TOYAMA DAIICHI HOTEL-BAR
b: Toyama Pref.
c: Nihon Sekkei Office Co., Ltd.
d: Takae Kondo
e: Takae Kondo

a: 富山第一ホテル レストラン
b: 富山県
c: 株式会社日本設計事務所
d: 近藤喬枝
e: 近藤喬枝

a: TOYAMA DAIICHI HOTEL-RESTAURANT
b: Toyama Pref.
c: Nihon Sekkei Office Co., Ltd.
d: Takae Kondo
e: Takae Kondo

a: レストラン けやき
b: マレーシア
c: 株式会社東急設計コンサルタント/株式会社降幡建築設計事務所
d: 大平善生
e: アトリエボノム/大平善生
●
a: RESTAURANT KEYAKI
b: Malaysia
c: Tokyu Sekkei Consultant/Furihata Architectural Office
d: Zensei Ohira
e: Atelier Bonhomme/Zensei Ohira

a: 今井浜 東急リゾート 和風レストラン
b: 静岡県河津町今井浜
c: 株式会社東急設計コンサルタント/株式会社降幡建築設計事務所
d: 猪口栄一
e: アトリエボノム/大平善生
●
a: IMAIHAMA TOKYU RESORT-JAPANESE RESTAURANT
b: Imaihama, Kawazu-cho, Sizuoka Pref.
c: Tokyu Sekkei Consultant/Furihata Architectural Office
d: Eiichi Iguchi
e: Atelier Bonhomme/Zensei Ohira

『ガッシュとエアブラシの混合描法』
進士竜一

◐

"The Combined Drawing Method of Gouache and Airbrush"
by Ryuichi Shinji

物件名❖クレプスキュール
Project Title❖CRÉPUSCULE

作画者❖進士竜一
Renderer❖Ryuichi Shinji

住所❖〒113 東京都文京区本駒込5-67-1クレール駒込511
Address❖511, Clair-Komagome, 5-67-1, Hon-Komagome, Bunkyo-ku,
Tokyo, 113　Tel.❖03-943-8345

01 今回は図面がないいわゆるイメージ・パースなので,このラフスケッチを基に製作を始める。これは美しい夜景の見えるレストランという想定で,様式的な造形と広いガラス面を特徴とするものだ。天井面を大きくとったのは,円蓋内部を見せるためであり,ここにはフレスコ画と天窓を配置する。

02 「イラストボードにスケッチを写す」スケッチの原画を方眼で分割し,描き写すという古典的な方法をとった。垂直線以外はほとんどフリーハンドで描き上げたので,かなり乱雑な下図となったが,細かい狂いは着色の段階で修正する。

03 「マスキングフィルムを貼る」マスキングフィルムは,トリコン製の強粘着タイプSP200を使用。中央から四方に向けて,空気やしわが入らぬよう注意深く密着する。

04 「カッティング」基本的には広い面積から着色していく。床面のマスキングフィルムを,下図の曖昧な線を修正するつもりでカットする。カッティングの精密さで,エアブラシの仕上りが左右されるので,慎重に行なうこと。切り取ったフィルムは,適当な紙に軽く貼りつけてとっておく。

05 「着彩」カーペットの下塗りには,アズールブルー,ウルトラマリン,ライト(いずれもニッカーのガッシュ)を使用。白のガッシュと混ぜて調整する。平筆でムラの出ないように,均一に素早く塗る。この時平滑な塗布面ができないと,エアブラシにムラが出てしまうので要注意。なお使用した絵具については,以下ニッカー製を(N),ターナー製を(T),ウィンザーニュートン製を(W),ホルベイン製を(H)として示す。又はメーカー表示のみの場合はガッシュ,透明水彩の場合は,その都度(透明)と記すこととする。

06 「エアブラシ」調合した色を,ためし吹きで確認する。ウルトラマリン・ライト(N),ローヤルパープル(N)を使用。

07 エアブラシを使う利点は,無段階の濃淡(グラデーション)が容易につけられることと,もう一つは,粒子の粗さを調節して物の材質感を表現できるという点だ。カーペットの手前の方を粗く吹いて遠近感,テクスチュアを表現する。

08 「色調チェック」マスキングで覆った周囲の絵具を拭き取り,色の変化を確認する。この作業は,以下の吹きつけの各プロセスにおいて,必ず行なう。

09 吹きつけの第一段階絨緞の地塗り終了。

10 「エアブラシ・砂吹き」砂吹きはエアブラシの重要なテクニックの一つ。コンプレッサーの圧力調節器,又はハンドピースのレバーの微妙な指加減で行なう。(ハンドピースによってはレバーの調節機能のついたものもあり,又はノズルによっても調節はできる)

11 黒(T)でカーペットの手前部分を砂吹きして,質感を強調する。

12 吹き終えたら,エアブラシ面にトリパブA(水性絵具定着液)をかける。ガッシュをエアブラシで使用しているので,そのままでは次にマスキングフィルムを貼ることができない。トリパブは表面の定着性の弱いガッシュの性質を補うもので,塗布面はマスキングフィルムともなじみ,手で触れても絵具の落ちる心配がないので,後の作業も容易となる。※トリパブの吹きすぎは絵の調子をくずす恐れがあるので注意。

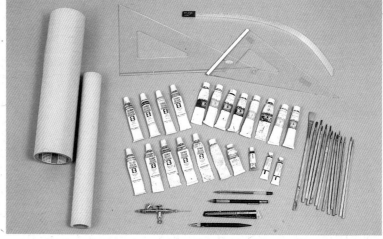

写真左上から。ライトブルー(ターナー),ジェットブラック(ターナー),ホワイト(ターナー),ディープグリーン(ターナー),ウルトラマリンライト(ニッカー),アズールブルー(ニッカー),ローヤルパープル(ニッカー),バイオレットジョンブリアン(ニッカー),バーントアンバー(ニッカー),ローングリーン(ニッカー),イエローオーカー(ニッカー)。
写真左下から。エメラルドグリーン(ターナー),ピンク(ターナー),バーントシェンナ(ターナー),パーマネントグリーンディープ(ターナー),シャトルーズ(ニッカー),ロウシェンナ(ニッカー),カーマイン(ホルベイン),バーントアンバー(ウィンザー&ニュートン)。

From top-left to right:Ligh Blue(Turner),Jet Black(Turner),
White(Turner),Deep Green(Turner),Ultra-marine Light(Nicker),
Azure Blue(Nicker),Royal Purple(Nicker),Violet(Nicker),Jaune Brillant(Nicker),
Burnt Umber(Nicker),Lawn Green(Nicker),Yellow Ochre(Nicker).
From bottom-left to right:Emerald Green(Turner),Pink(Turner),
Burnt Sienna(Turner),Permanent Green Deep(Turner),
Chartreuse(Nicker),Raw Sienna(Nicker),
Below are the transparent colors:Carmine(Holbein),Burnt Umber(Windsor & Newton).

01 This rough sketch is used as the original base for the so-called perspective drawing as the actual plan is not available. The stylish modelling and wide windows are distiguishing here as the model is a restaurant with a night scene as a backdrop. A large amount of space was taken for the ceiling in order to display the vaulted interior. The fresco and skylight will be laid out in this area.

02 Copy this sketch onto the illustration board. Apart from the vertical lines, the sketch is hand-drawn which makes the drawing quite rough, but the details will be altered during the coloring stage.

03 Apply a masking film to the drawing. The masking film used here is of Toricon make and is a strong adhesive SP200 type. Carefully apply the film from the centre in all directions and press out all air bubbles and creases.

04 Cutting. Basically the coloring will commence from the wide-open areas. Cut out the masking surface in order to correct the unclear lines on the sketch. As the end result of the airbrushing will depend on the accuracy of the cutting proccess, a great deal of care should be taken here. The cut-out portions of film should be lightly stuck onto a spare piece of paper for later use.

05 Coloring. Azure blue and ultra-marine of Nicker's gouache are used for the undercoat of the carpet. The colors may be controlled by adding white to the gouache. Paint swiftly and evenly without leaving any patches with the use of a flat brush. This will require special attention as the airbrush will leave patches on any uneven surfaces. Hereinafter the makes of airbrushes will be abbreviated to the following: Nicker=(N), Windsor & Newton=(W), Holbein=(H). Additionally, individual makers will be indicated simply as gouache and transparent colors will be known as transparents.

06 Airbrush. Test the spray. Use ultra-marine (N) and royal purple (N).

07 The advantages of using an airbrush are the capability of simplifying the uncontrollable stages of color graduation, and expressing the texture of materials by controlling the size of the particles. The distance is of expressed by spraying coures particles of paint onto the fore of the carpet.

08 Check the color tones. Wipe away the excess paint on the masking surface in order to confirm the change in color. This must be repeated at each stage of spraying.

09 The first coat of the carpet. The initial step is complete.

10 Airbrush sand blasting. Sand blasting is considered to be one of the most important techniques of airbrushing. This is done by the use of the pressure controller on the compressor or the finger adjustments on the hand-piece lever (some hand-pieces have lever adjustment functions and some are adjusted by the nozzle).

11 Sand blasting is applied on the fore section of the carpet with the use of black (T) in order to emphasize the texture.

12 Once the airbrushing is finished, Tripub (water-paint fixing solution) is sprayed onto the airbrushed surface. As gouache is used here for airbrushing, masking film cannot be applied onto the surface without the processing. Tripub-A supplements the weak nature of the gouache by fixing the surface and lessening the problem of paint being stripped off by the application of the masking film. ∗ Caution: Care should be taken to avoid spraying on too much Tripabu as there is a chance that the tone of color may be spoilt.

進士竜一氏のアトリエ。
Mr. Ryuichi Shinji's atelier

13 「カーペットのパターンを描く」絵の上に直接白鉛筆で下描きする。遠近法にのっとり，丁寧に作図すること。下描きの線は，消ゴムで簡単に消せる程度に弱く描く。

14 「カーペット面の完成」パターンで遠近感が強調される。この上から切り取っておいたマスキングフィルムを，寸分のズレもないように，慎重に貼りもどす。以下このマスキングシートでの部分描きの場合は，この作業をくり返す。

15 「室外の空を塗る」夕暮れを想定しているので，空の色は低空を赤紫に，上空を向うにつれてウルトラマリンとする。明るい赤系から暗い青系の変化は，逆色相移行となるので，特に中空部の色は大変濁りやすい。予めの緻密な色彩計画が必要である。下塗りは簡単にグラデーションをつけておく。絵具はライラック(T)，ウルトラマリンライト(N)を使用。

16 低空と中空の境いは，薄く吹く。必要以上に濃くなると，後に吹きつけるウルトラマリンと混色して濁ってしまう。絵具はピンク(T)とライラック(T)を使用。※エアブラシは一度で濃くしようとすると失敗しやすいので注意。マスキング中にドライヤーを使用する場合は冷風で。

17 中空をウルトラマリンライト(N)を薄めて，透明絵具に近い状態で吹き，低空につなぐ。上空に向うにつれ濃く吹き，紫を加える。最上空には黒を混ぜた。

18 「星を入れる」白(T)のごく粗い砂吹きで星を入れる。星の位置に偶然性を与えるため，絵からハンドピースをかなり離して，絵具の粒を落とす感じで吹く。他に網とブラシを使ったスパッタリングと言う方法もある。

19 「樹木を描く」外の樹木は，夕映えを美しく演出するため，輪郭の影としてとらえて描き込む。絵具はジェットブラック(T)と透明のカーマイン(H)を使用。低木は彩度を落としたブルーグリーンを使用。この場合目立たす必要はない。

20 「屋外の風景の仕上り」

21 「壁の下塗り」白に微量の黄を混ぜて塗る。その上からエアブラシで濃い色を吹いてゆく。絵具はホワイト(T)，シャトルーズ(N)，バーントシエナ(T)，ジョンブリアン(N)など。

22 「大理石の柱の着彩」明るい色で下塗りをしてから模様を入れる。薄い色で全体の石目の流れを入れてから，徐々に濃い色で細かい模様を入れ，密度を上げる。大理石のような変成岩には様々な色とそれぞれの特長的な模様があるので注意すること。

23 「質感を描く」大理石の模様を入れてから，エアブラシで立体感を出す。美しく磨き上げられた石の透明感を損なわぬよう注意する。さらに全体の調子を見て，光の方向を確認してからハイライトを入れる。絵具はイエローオーカー(N)，バーントシエナ(T)，透明のバーントアンバーなど使用。

24 「天井を描く」大きな面を占める天井に，どのような役割を与えるかで，絵全体の印象が大きく変わる。全体の面構成を十分に考慮した上で，色を決める。

25 円蓋内部の半分は，フレスコ画とする。フレスコ画独特の淡い色調で仕上げる。

26 「天井部の装飾」溝引きの入った定規を使い面相筆で描き込む。

27 「天井面の仕上り」円蓋を2重に間接照明がとりまく。フレスコ画は絵の中の絵となるので，弱感の曖昧さが必要だろう。

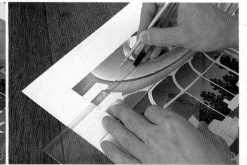

13 Draw in the carpet's pattern. Draw the sketches directly onto the top of the actual picture with the use of a white pencil. Ensure that the drawing is done neatly with the use of the perspective method. Each line should be drawn lightly to simplify the rubbing out with an eraser.

14 The completion of the carpet surface. The pattern emphasizes the feeling of distance. The pieces of masking film cut out earlier and carefully retained may now be stuck back into their original places without leaving any gaps. This same process should be continued throughout the painting.

15 Paint in the outside sky. As this drawing assumes the evening twighlight the lower part of the sky shuold be painted in purplish red turning into ultra-marine as it moves upwards. As this extreme change from light-red to dark-blue is a reverse hue translation, the colors shuold be merged where they meet. The thorough planning of color schemes must be carried out before-hand. The undercoat graduation should use lilac (T) and ultra-marine (W).

16 Lightly spray in the border of the lower and middle section of the sky. If it seems too dark it will get mixed with the ultramarine that will be sprayed on later. Pink (T) and lilac (T) should be used here. ＊Caution: Care should be taken to ensure that too much dark color is not sprayed on it one go. When using a dryer, the temperature should be set on cold air.

17 This down the ultra-marine (N) until it reaches a transparent color and spray it onto the middle sky in order to link it with the lower sky. As you reach the upper area of sky add purple to make it darker. Black was used here to complete the topmost sky area.

18 Insert the stars. The stars are added by applying white course sand blasting to give it a random effect with the hand-piece held some distance above the surface to allow the drops of paint to drip onto the picture. Another method of using a net and brush and known as spattering may be utilized.

19 Drawing the trees. The outside trees are drawn as shadows against the skyline to produce the effect of a beautiful sunset. Black (T) and transparent carmine (H) are used here. The lighter blue-green is used for the bushes. In this case there is no necessity to distinguish them.

20 The completion of the outside view.

21 The undercoat of the wall. The wall is painted white with a touch of yellow. Darker colors will then be sprayed over. White (T), chartreus (N), burnt sienna (T) and jaune brilliant should be used for the colors.

22 Coloring the granite pillar. The pattern should be painted on after the first coat of bright paint. Once the flow of the stone grain is painted on in a lighter color, the detail should be picked out in a darker color to increase the density. Attention should be paid to the metamorphic quality of the rock which has vari ous colors and distinguishing patterns.

23 Drawing the quality. The solid look is added by the airbrush after the pattern of the granite is pained on. Be careful not to spoil the transparent look of the beautifully polished stone. Highlights should be added after having studied the whole balance and the direction of the light. Yellow ocre (N), burnt sienna (T) and transparent burnt umber should be used for the colors.

24 Drawing the ceiling. The final impression of the picture as a whole will depend greatly on the role of the ceiling that takes quite a large area of the scene. The colors should be decided upon after thorough consideration of the over-all sectional formation.

25 Half of the vaulted area should be filled with the fresco. The light tones of typical frescos should be used.

26 Ceiling decorations. Paint with the use of a grooved ruler and a countenance brush.

27 Completion of the ceiling. The indirect lighting surrounds the vaulted ceiling twice. As the fresco will become a painting within a painting, a certain amount of vagueness is necessary.

28 柱頭部。この部分も溝引きで描く。焦点のとれない場合は定規の方向性を慎重に決めていく。

29 「金箔を貼った装飾」金の表現は，色と光の変化を強く出す。つまり黄系から赤系への変化。白いハイライトから黒い影への変化となる。面相又は細ゴシック筆などでフリーハンドで慎重に描き込む。使用した絵具はシャトルーズ（N），ローアンバー（N），バーントシエナ（T），透明のセピア（H）など。

30 柱の仕上り。

31 「窓枠のR部分に陰を入れる」この程度のRは，手首を軸にして指先を回転させるように，フリーハンドで描く。絵具のふくみ，筆先のコントロールに注意。

32 「窓枠にエアブラシでグラデーションをつける」

33 「床木部の下塗り」イエローオーカー（N），ローシエナ（W）で明るめに塗る。この色は最終的に床の反射面の色として残るので暗くならない様に。

34 「木目を描く」面相筆の先をばらし，溝引きで木目を入れてゆく。

35 木目を描いた上から，エアブラシで濃い色を吹きつける。濃くなるにつれて，赤味を強くしてゆく。

36 全体のグラデーションをつけてから，楽器類の影を吹きつけて，床平面を仕上げる。

37 「家具を描く」同様のプロセスを経て，楽器と家具の面をつくる。細かいディティールは，最も神経を要する作業なので，最終の仕上げ行程にまわす。

38 椅子は，まず中間となる色で全体を描き，次に陰となる部分，明るい部分，影，ハイライトと段階的に仕上げる。絵具はバーントシエナを中心に。

39 「椅子とテーブルの仕上がり」影の流れ，ハイライトを正確に描く事によって光の方向性を明確にし，絵により臨場感を与える。

40 「楽器を描く」この部分では，床・チェンバロ・チェロと三つの木質が重なるので，個々の存在を明確にするため，少しづつ色調を変える必要があるだろう。

41 ディティールを描き込み，楽器を仕上げる。まだ木質の印象が弱いので，色調整の必要があるが，全体の調子を見ながら完成させる。

42 「添景を残しての部屋の仕上がり」

43 「大理石製の花台を描く」柱同様大理石の層状模様と本磨きの質感に注意。

44 「添景を描く」全体に紫の印象が強いので，補色となる緑は，色構成の上においても効果的に配さなければならない。面相筆などで，ていねいに描く。仕上りに近づくにつれ作業は楽しいものとなるが，全体のバランスを見ながら色相には注意して描き込もう。

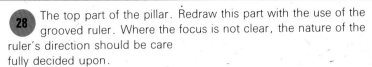

28 The top part of the pillar. Redraw this part with the use of the grooved ruler. Where the focus is not clear, the nature of the ruler's direction should be care fully decided upon.

29 Gold-plated decorations. A change in color and light is used to emphasize and express the gold look. This is a direct change from white highlights to black shadow. The face of the pillar should be carefully drawn by hand with gothic lettering. The colors to be chosen are chartreuse (N), raw umber (N), burnt sienna (T) and transparent sepia.

30 The completed pillar.

31 Place the shade around the window frames. The circle areas should be drawn by hand using the finger-tips and wrist as the axis. Pay attention to the quantity of paint used and the control of the brush tip.

32 Make the graduations of the frame-work by brush.

33 Undercoating the wooden floor. Paint the floor with bright colors such as yellow ocre (N) and raw sienna (W). As these colors will remain as the reflections on the floor, care should be taken to ensure that they are too dark.

34 Drawing the wood grain. The tip of the countenance should be seperated and the wood grian drawn in with the use of a grooved ruler.

35 Airbrush on a darker color to the top of the wood graining. Add more red coloring as it gets darker.

36 After the over-all graduation has been added, spray on the shadows of the instruments and finish the floor plane surface.

37 Drawing the furniture. The surface of the musical instrument and the furniture should be made using the same process. The fine details must be left to the very end as they involve very delicate work.

38 Initially natural coloring should be used on the chair.

39 The completion of the chairs and tables. A clear grasp of the light direction is necessary in order to add the flow of the shade and highlights and add the presence needed.

40 Drawing the instruments. As three kinds of wooden textures — the floor, the cembalo and the cello — are to be painted here, the tone of the colors should be slightly altered in order to clarify their identity.

41 Putting in the detail. Complete the instruments. As the wooden texture is not yet expressed well here, color adjustment is still needed but the process should be completed by studying the harmony of the whole picture.

42 The room is complete except from the human interest items.

43 Drawing the flower stand. Pay a similar attention to the stratified pattern and the polished looks of the granite stone as was paid to the pillars.

44 Adding the human interest. As purple represents the color of this picture on the whole, the complimentary green should be effectively arranged for the sake of the color structure. Draw carefully with the use of the countenace brush. This process becomes quite enjoyable as the picture draws near to completion, but the color tones should be attended to carefully by observing the balance of the whole picture.

45　テーブル上の食器類は，レストランの華やいだ雰囲気を演出するための重要な小道具だ。食器の種類によって店の性格を説明できるので，緻密に描き込む必要がある。心地良いざわめきさえも予感させれば，成功といえるだろう。

46　レストランに飾る絵画は，あまり重苦しくならない方が良い。食器類等と同様，店の雰囲気に合うものを選ぶ。

47　花の色は，背景の色とのバランスを考えて描き込む。

48　木部に色修正を施して仕上げる。

49　月にクレーター，山影等を入れて，これで全行程の完了とする。

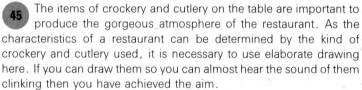

45　The items of crockery and cutlery on the table are important to produce the gorgeous atmosphere of the restaurant. As the characteristics of a restaurant can be determined by the kind of crockery and cutlery used, it is necessary to use elaborate drawing here. If you can draw them so you can almost hear the sound of them clinking then you have achieved the aim.

46　Heavy painting are not recommendable for restaurants. The paintings should be selected to suit the atmosphere like the cutlery and crockery.

47　The colors in the picture should be decided in accordance to the balnce of the colors available in the views.

48　Add the final touches to the wooden surfaces.

49　The craters and shadows on the moon are added to complete the entire process of the picture.

3. 販売専門店　3. Retail Stores

ホテル内店舗
ショッピング・センター
ショールーム
ブティック
薬局
電器店
眼鏡店
美容院
ゲーム・ランド
スポーツ・ショップ
フラワー・ショップ
各種店舗……他

Shop in Hotel
Shopping Center
Showroom
Boutique
Drugstore
Electrical Shop
Optician
Beauty Salon
Game Center
Sport Shop
Flower Shop
Various Shops……etc.

a: ホテルモントレー神戸A
b: 兵庫県神戸市
c: 鹿島建設建築設計本部
e: 鹿島建設株式会社
●
a: HOTEL MONTOLEY KOBE A
b: Kobe-shi, Hyogo Pref.
c: Kajima Corporation Architectural Design Division
e: Kajima Corporation

a: ホテルモントレー神戸B
b: 兵庫県神戸市
c: 鹿島建設建築設計本部
e: 鹿島建設株式会社

a: HOTEL MONTOLEY KOBE B
b: Kobe-shi, Hyogo Pref.
c: Kajima Corporation Architectural Design Division
e: Kajima Corporation

a: 第一滝本館
b: 北海道登別市
c: 鹿島建設建築設計本部
e: 鹿島建設株式会社

a: DAIICHI TAKIMOTOKAN
b: Noboribetsu-shi, Hokkaido
c: Kajima Corporation Architectural Design Division
e: Kajima Corporation

a: ホテル日航福岡
b: 福岡県福岡市
c: 鹿島建設建築設計本部
e: 鹿島建設株式会社

a: HOTEL NIKKO FUKUOKA
b: Fukuoka-shi, Fukuoka Pref.
c: Kajima Corporation Architectural Design Division
e: Kajima Corporation

a: 札幌日通ホテル
b: 北海道札幌市
c: 鹿島建設建築設計本部
e: 鹿島建設株式会社
●
a: SAPPORO NITTSU HOTEL
b: Sapporo-shi, Hokkaido
c: Kajima Corporation Architectural Design Division
e: Kajima Corporation

a: ロイヤルパークホテル高松
b: 香川県高松市
c: 株式会社穴吹工務店
d: 金本正
e: 金本正
●
a: ROYAL PARK HOTEL TAKAMATSU
b: Takamatsu-shi, Kagawa Pref.
c: Anabuki Komuten Co., Ltd.
d: Tadashi Kanemoto
e: Tadashi Kanemoto

a: キャピタルホテル1000
b: 岩手県陸前高田市
c: 株式会社アーバンライフ建築事務所
d: 小林未浩
e: 株式会社オズ・アトリエ

●
a: CAPITAL HOTEL 1000
b: Rikuzen-Takada-shi, Iwate Pref.
c: Urban Life Architect & Associates Inc.
d: Mihiro Kobayashi
e: OZ-Atelier Co., Ltd.

a: 道後温泉観光会館
b: 愛媛県松山市
c: 玉乃井公和建築事務所
d: 川嶋俊介/中矢守
e: 川嶋俊介
●
a: DOGO SPA SIGHTSEEING INFORMATION CENTER
b: Matsuyama-shi, Ehime Pref.
c: Masakazu Tamanoi & Architects
d: Shunsuke Kawashima/Mamoru Nakaya
e: Shunsuke Kawashima

a: 比羅満都
b: 北海道上富良野町
c: A.H.O.pro
d: 桑田謹次
e: 伊東剛

a: PYRAMID
b: Kami-Furano-cho, Hokkaido
c: A.H.O.pro
d: Kinji Kuwata
e: Go Ito

a: ショップビル シーン
b: 東京都
c: アヅチ・プランニングスタジオ
d: 安土実
e: 安土実

● a: SHOP BUILDING SEEN
b: Tokyo
c: Azuchi Planning Studio
d: Minoru Azuchi
e: Minoru Azuchi

a: ショッピングモールATAMI
b: 静岡県熱海市
c: テツ・クリエイティブ
d: 安土実
e: 安土実
●
a: SHOPPING MOLE ATAMI
b: Atami-shi, Shizuoka Pref.
c: Testu Creaitive
d: Minoru Azuchi
e: Minoru Azuchi

a: ショッピングセンター
c: 田中設計事務所
d: 奥村一也
e: 有限会社ヒューマン・ファクター

a: SHOPPING CENTER PLAN
c: Tanaka Architectual Design Co., Ltd.
d: Kazuya Okumura
e: Human Factor Ltd.

a: ショッピングセンター　アトリウム
c: 株式会社布谷
d: ハタスペース株式会社
e: ハタスペース株式会社/秦昜八

a: SHOPPING CENTER ATRIUM
c: Nunotani Co., Ltd.
d: Hata Space Co., Ltd.
e: Hata Space Co., Ltd./Shohachi Hata

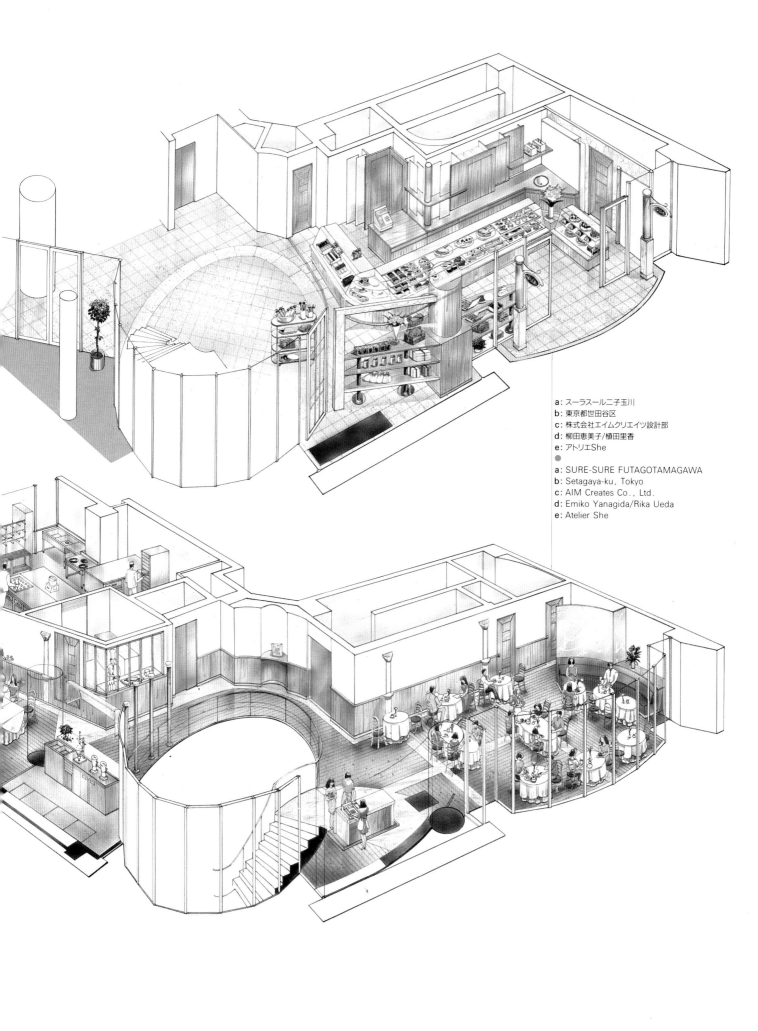

a: スーラスール二子玉川
b: 東京都世田谷区
c: 株式会社エイムクリエイツ設計部
d: 柳田恵美子/植田里香
e: アトリエShe

a: SURE-SURE FUTAGOTAMAGAWA
b: Setagaya-ku, Tokyo
c: AIM Creates Co., Ltd.
d: Emiko Yanagida/Rika Ueda
e: Atelier She

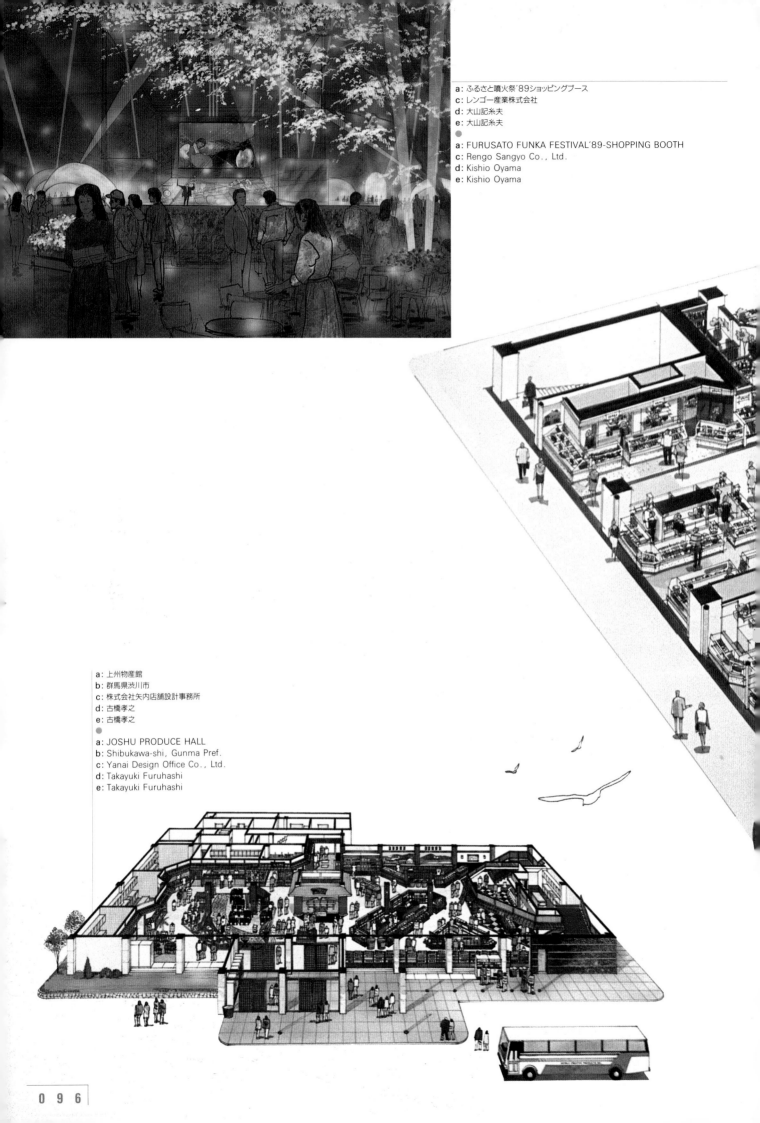

a: ふるさと噴火祭'89ショッピングブース
c: レンゴー産業株式会社
d: 大山記糸夫
e: 大山記糸夫
●
a: FURUSATO FUNKA FESTIVAL'89-SHOPPING BOOTH
c: Rengo Sangyo Co., Ltd.
d: Kishio Oyama
e: Kishio Oyama

a: 上州物産館
b: 群馬県渋川市
c: 株式会社矢内店舗設計事務所
d: 古橋孝之
e: 古橋孝之
●
a: JOSHU PRODUCE HALL
b: Shibukawa-shi, Gunma Pref.
c: Yanai Design Office Co., Ltd.
d: Takayuki Furuhashi
e: Takayuki Furuhashi

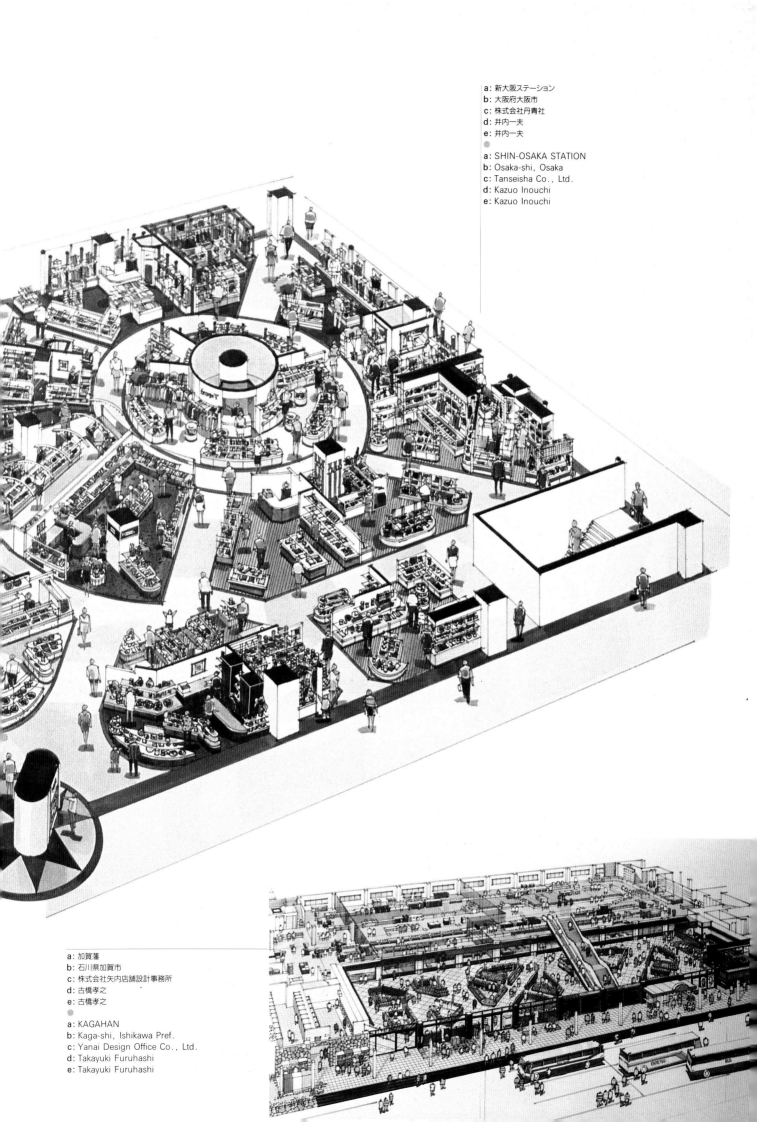

a: 新大阪ステーション
b: 大阪府大阪市
c: 株式会社丹青社
d: 井内一夫
e: 井内一夫

a: SHIN-OSAKA STATION
b: Osaka-shi, Osaka
c: Tanseisha Co., Ltd.
d: Kazuo Inouchi
e: Kazuo Inouchi

a: 加賀藩
b: 石川県加賀市
c: 株式会社矢内店舗設計事務所
d: 古橋孝之
e: 古橋孝之

a: KAGAHAN
b: Kaga-shi, Ishikawa Pref.
c: Yanai Design Office Co., Ltd.
d: Takayuki Furuhashi
e: Takayuki Furuhashi

a: ワールドトラベルフェア
b: 東京都豊島区池袋
c: オムニバス
d: 安土実
e: 安土実

a: WORLD TRAVEL FAIR
b: Ikebukuro, Toshima-ku, Tokyo
c: Omunibus
d: Minoru Azuchi
e: Minoru Azuchi

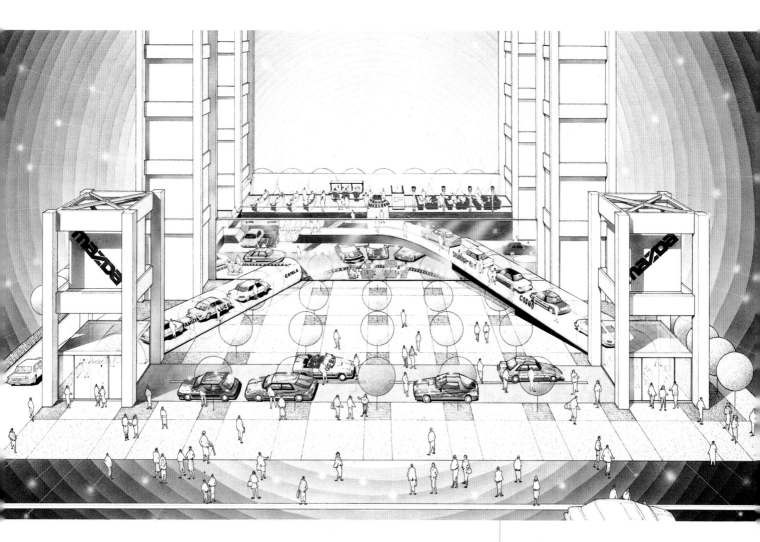

a: マツダ勝どき6丁目
b: 東京都中央区
c: 鹿島建設建築設計本部
e: 鹿島建設株式会社

a: MATSUDA KACHIDOKI 6-CHOME
b: Chuo-ku, Tokyo
c: Kajima Corporation Architectural Design Division
e: Kajima Corporation

a: サンゲツのショールーム
b: 愛知県名古屋市
c: カトウ美装株式会社
d: 譚少芝
e: 譚少芝
●
a: SANGETSU SHOWROOM
b: Nagoya-shi, Aichi Pref.
c: Kato Biso CO., LTD.
d: Tan Shao Zhi
e: Tan Shao Zhi

a: MICROAGEショールーム
b: 愛知県名古屋市
c: カトウ美装株式会社
d: 譚少芝
e: 譚少芝

a: MICROAGE SHOWROOM
b: Nagoya-shi, Aichi Pref.
c: Kato Biso Co., Ltd.
d: Tan Shao Zhi
e: Tan Shao Zhi

a: 神奈川トヨタ伊勢原営業所
b: 神奈川県伊勢原市
c: 株式会社中西設計事務所
d: アカサカレンダリング
e: 赤坂孝史

a: KANAGAWA TOYOTA-ISEHARA SHOWROOM
b: Isehara-shi, Kanagawa Pref.
c: Nakanishi Architectural Design Co., Ltd.
d: Akasaka Rendering
e: Takashi Akasaka

a: 群馬トヨタ前橋営業所
b: 群馬県前橋市
c: 隈研吾/CAD計画研究所
d: 諏訪利弘/スワデザイン
e: 諏訪利弘

a: GUNMA TOYOTA-MAEBASHI SHOWROOM
b: Maebashi-shi, Gunma Pref.
c: Kengo Kuma/CAD Institution Planning Inc.
d: Toshihiro Suwa/Suwa Design
e: Toshihiro Suwa

a: 大阪トヨペット箕面ショールーム
b: 大阪府箕面市
c: 新和建設株式会社/ハタスペース株式会社
d: ハタスペース株式会社/秦昇八
e: ハタスペース株式会社/秦昇八

a: OSAKA TOYOPET-MINOO SHOWROOM
b: Minoo-shi, Osaka
c: Shinwa Kensetsu Co., Ltd./Hata Space Co., Ltd.
d: Hata Space Co., Ltd./Shohachi Hata
e: Hata Space Co., Ltd./Shohachi Hata

a: 原宿クエスト
b: 東京都渋谷区神宮前
c: NTT都市開発株式会社
d: 長尾恵美子
e: 長尾恵美子

a: HARAJUKU QUWST
b: Jingumae, Shibuya-ku, Tokyo
c: NTT Toshikaihastu Co., Ltd.
d: Emiko Nagao
e: Emiko Nagao

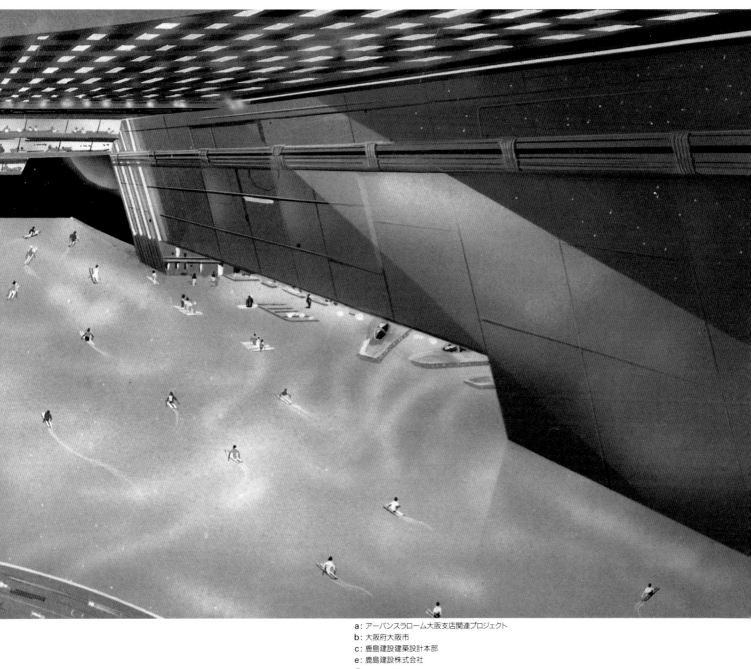

a: アーバンスラローム大阪支店関連プロジェクト
b: 大阪府大阪市
c: 鹿島建設建築設計本部
e: 鹿島建設株式会社

a: URBAN SLALOM OSAKA BRANCH PROJECT
b: Osaka-shi, Osaka
c: Kajima Corporation Architectural Design Division
e: Kajima Corporation

a: インターメッツォ メンズショップ
b: 大阪府大阪市
c: 株式会社ダーバン
d: 井内一夫
e: 井内一夫

a: INTERMEZZO MEN'S SHOP
b: Osaka-shi, Osaka
c: Durban Co., Ltd.
d: Kazuo Inouchi
e: Kazuo Inouchi

a: ダーバン メンズショップ
b: 大阪府大阪市
c: 株式会社ダーバン
d: 井内一夫
e: 井内一夫

a: DURBAN MEN'S SHOP
b: Osaka-shi, Osaka
c: Durban Co., Ltd.
d: Kazuo Inouchi
e: Kazuo Inouchi

a: ブティックエルザ
b: 兵庫県神戸市
c: 株式会社クリエイトセンター
d: 松村範也
e: 株式会社レンダリングウルフ

a: BOUTIQUE ELSA
b: Kobe-shi, Hyogo Pref.
c: Create Center Co., Ltd.
d: Noriya Matsumura
e: Rendering WOLF Co., Ltd.

a: リカーブティック
b: 愛知県名古屋市
c: 株式会社アートステージ
d: 大山記糸夫
e: 大山記糸夫

a: LIQUOR BOTIQUE
b: Nagoya-shi, Aichi Pref.
c: Art Stage Co., Ltd.
d: Kishio Oyama
e: Kishio Oyama

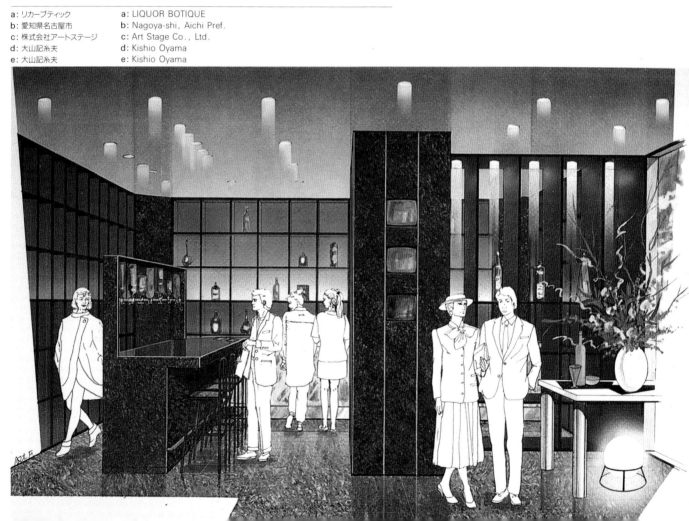

a: ウエディングサービス ワタベ
b: 東京都中央区日本橋
c: 株式会社矢内店舗設計事務所
d: 古橋孝之
e: 古橋孝之
●
a: WEDDING SERVICE WATABE
b: Nihonbashi, Chuo-ku, Tokyo
c: Yanai Design Office Co., Ltd.
d: Takayuki Furuhashi
e: Takayuki Furuhashi

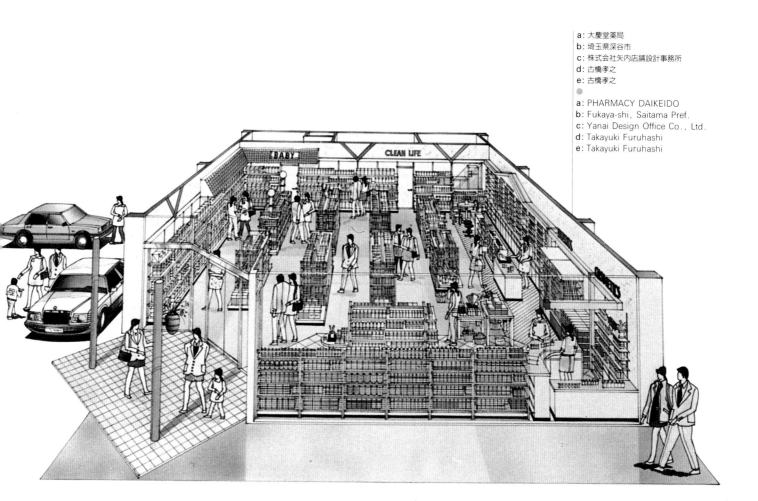

a: 大慶堂薬局
b: 埼玉県深谷市
c: 株式会社矢内店舗設計事務所
d: 古橋孝之
e: 古橋孝之

a: PHARMACY DAIKEIDO
b: Fukaya-shi, Saitama Pref.
c: Yanai Design Office Co., Ltd.
d: Takayuki Furuhashi
e: Takayuki Furuhashi

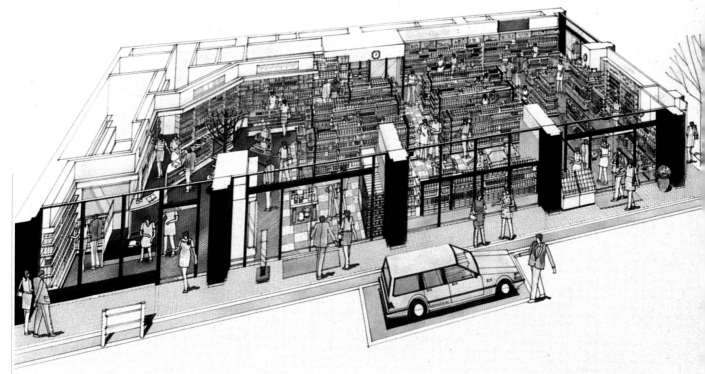

a: ニシザワ薬局
b: 東京都千代田区
c: 株式会社矢内店舗設計事務所
d: 古橋孝之
e: 古橋孝之

a: PHARMACY NISHIZAWA
b: Chiyoda-ku, Tokyo
c: Yanai Design Office Co., Ltd.
d: Takayuki Furuhashi
e: Takayuki Furuhashi

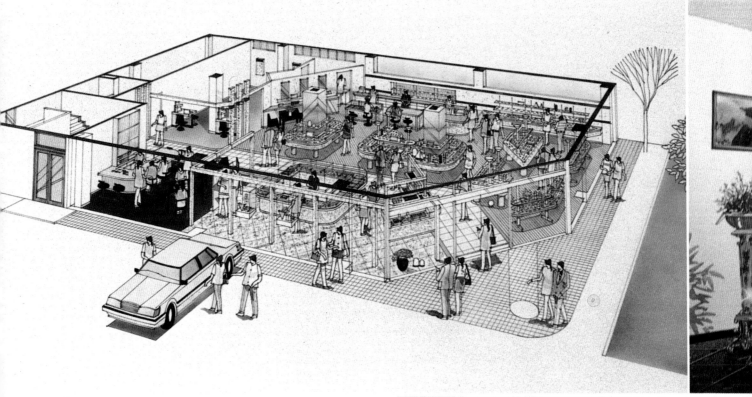

a: カンダメガネ
b: 岡山県津山市
c: 株式会社矢内店舗設計事務所
d: 古橋孝之
e: 古橋孝之

●

a: OPTICAL KANDA
b: Tsuyama-shi, Okayama Pref.
c: Yanai Design Office Co., Ltd.
d: Takayuki Furuhashi
e: Takayuki Furuhashi

a: 電気店
b: 兵庫県姫路市
c: 株式会社オオタ工芸
d: 隼デザイン事務所/四海隼一
e: 四海隼一

●

a: ELECTRICAL APPLIANCES STORE
b: Himeji-shi, Hyogo Pref.
c: Ota Kogei Ltd.
d: Hayabusa Design Office/Shunichi Shikai
e: Shunichi Shikai

a: 美容室
b: 大阪府大阪市
d: 湯浅禎也
e: 株式会社コラム・デザインセンター

a: BEAUTY SALON
b: Osaka-shi, Osaka
d: Yoshiya Yuasa
e: Column Design Center Inc.

a: ビューティー青山
b: 宮城県仙台市
c: 株式会社潤建築工房
d: 庄司澄子
e: 庄司澄子

a: BEAUTY AOYAMA PLAN
b: Sendai-shi, Miyagi Pref.
c: JUN Architectural Design Office
d: Sumiko Shoji
e: Sumiko Shoji

a: 六本木V　　　　　　a: ROPPONGI-V PLAN
b: 東京都港区六本木　　b: Roppongi, Minato-ku, Tokyo
c: C.D.W.ジパング　　　c: C.D.W.JIPANG
d: 柳川敏行　　　　　　d: Toshiyuki Yanagawa
e: 柳川敏行　　　　　　e: Toshiyuki Yanagawa

a: 美容院
b: 兵庫県姫路市
c: 株式会社オオタ工芸
d: 隼デザイン事務所/四海隼一
e: 四海隼一
●
a: BEAUTY SALON
b: Himeji-shi, Hyogo Pref.
c: Ota Kogei Ltd.
d: Hayabusa Design Office/Shunichi Shikai
e: Shunichi Shikai

a: ディスコ ケイズ
b: 宮城県仙台市
c: 株式会社エム・ディー
d: 加藤春枝
e: ケイズ

a: DISCO K'S
b: Sendai-shi, Miyagi Pref.
c: MD Co.
d: Harue Kato
e: Keiz

a: ゲームランド オーバン
b: 東京都渋谷区
c: アヅチ・プランニングスタジオ
d: 安土実
e: 安土実

a: GAME LAND OHBAN
b: Shibuya-ku, Tokyo
c: Azuchi Planning Studio
d: Minoru Azuchi
e: Minoru Azuchi

a: ディスコ ライラ
b: グァム
c: コンセプトキュー
d: 安土実
e: 安土実

a: DISCO LAYLA
b: Guam
c: Concept Kyu
d: Minoru Azuchi
e: Minoru Azuchi

a: ライブ・ディスコ2525
b: 京都府京都市
c: アヅチ・プランニングスタジオ
d: 安土実
e: 安土実

a: LIVE DISCO 2525
b: Kyoto-shi, Kyoto
c: Azuchi Planning Studio
d: Minoru Azuchi
e: Minoru Azuchi

a: イリュージョンディスコ ザバレス
b: 沖縄県那覇市
c: 株式会社エム・ディー
d: 加藤春枝
e: ケイズ

a: ILLUSION DISCO ZAVARES
b: Naha-shi, Okinawa Pref.
c: MD Co.
d: Harue Kato
e: Keiz

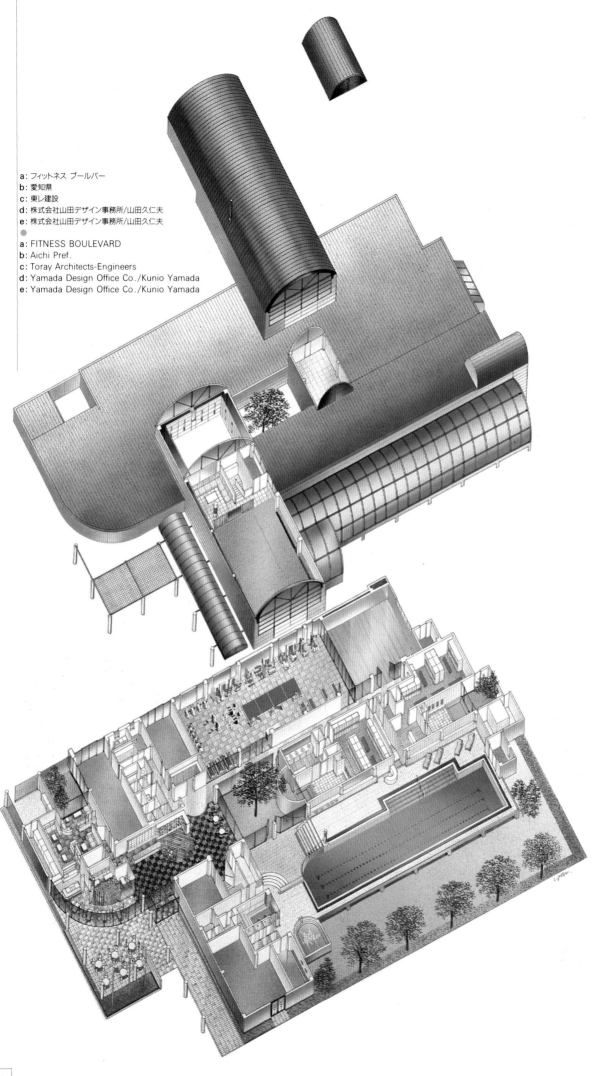

a: フィットネス プールバー
b: 愛知県
c: 東レ建設
d: 株式会社山田デザイン事務所/山田久仁夫
e: 株式会社山田デザイン事務所/山田久仁夫
●
a: FITNESS BOULEVARD
b: Aichi Pref.
c: Toray Architects-Engineers
d: Yamada Design Office Co./Kunio Yamada
e: Yamada Design Office Co./Kunio Yamada

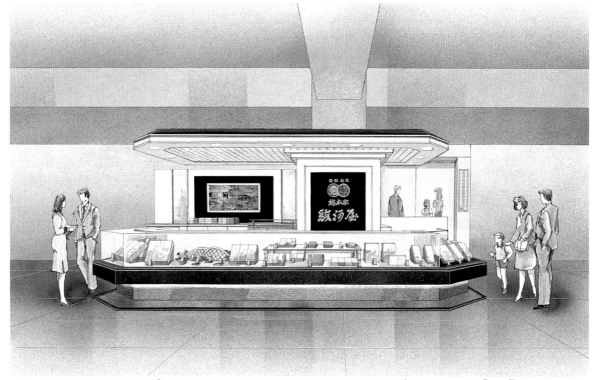

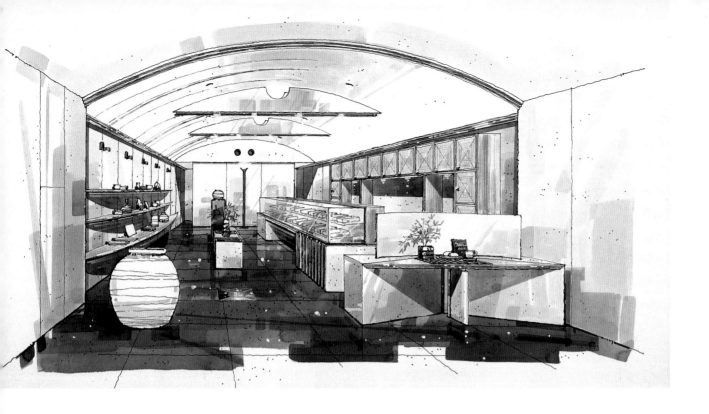

a: 総本家駿河屋B
b: 大阪府大阪市
c: 株式会社丸善店装
d: 松村範也
e: 株式会社レンダリングウルフ

a: THE HEAD SHOP OF SURUGAYA B
b: Osaka-shi, Osaka
c: Maruzen Tenso Co., Ltd.
d: Noriya Matsumura
e: Rendering WOLF Co., Ltd.

a: 白久プラン
b: 愛媛県松山市
c: 玉乃井公和建築事務所
d: 川嶋俊介/中矢守
e: 川嶋俊介

a: SHIRAKYU PLAN
b: Matsuyama-shi, Ehime Pref.
c: Masakazu Tamanoi & Architects
d: Shunsuke Kawashima/Mamoru Nakaya
e: Shunsuke Kawashima

a: オフィスのラウンジコーナー
d: 仲田貴代史
e: 株式会社コラム・デザインセンター

a: OFFICE-LOUNGE CORNER
d: Kiyoshi Nakata
e: Column Design Center Inc.

a: 春泰堂
b: 愛媛県砥部町
c: アトリエA&A
d: 川嶋俊介/中矢守
e: 川嶋俊介

a: SHUNTAIDO
b: Tobe-cho, Ehime Pref.
c: Atelier A&A
d: Shunsuke Kawashima/Mamoru Nakaya
e: Shunsuke Kawashima

a: フラワーギャラリー
c: 小野商会株式会社
d: 松村範也
e: 株式会社レンダリングウルフ

a: FLOWER GALLERY
c: Ono Shokai Co., Ltd.
d: Noriya Matsumura
e: Rendering WOLF Co., Ltd.

a: トヨタカローラ南海ショールーム
b: 大阪府貝塚市
c: 株式会社安部工務店
d: 芳野明
e: 芳野明

●

a: TOYOTA CAROLLA NANKAI SHOWROOM
b: Kaizuka-shi, Osaka
c: Abe Corporation
d: Akira Yoshino
e: Akira Yoshino

a: 花のモナミ
b: 埼玉県上尾市
c: 株式会社坂田建設
d: 大石敏雄
e: 大石敏雄

a: HANA NO MONAMI
b: Ageo-shi, Saitama Pref.
c: Sakata Construction Co., Ltd.
d: Toshio Oishi
e: Toshio Oishi

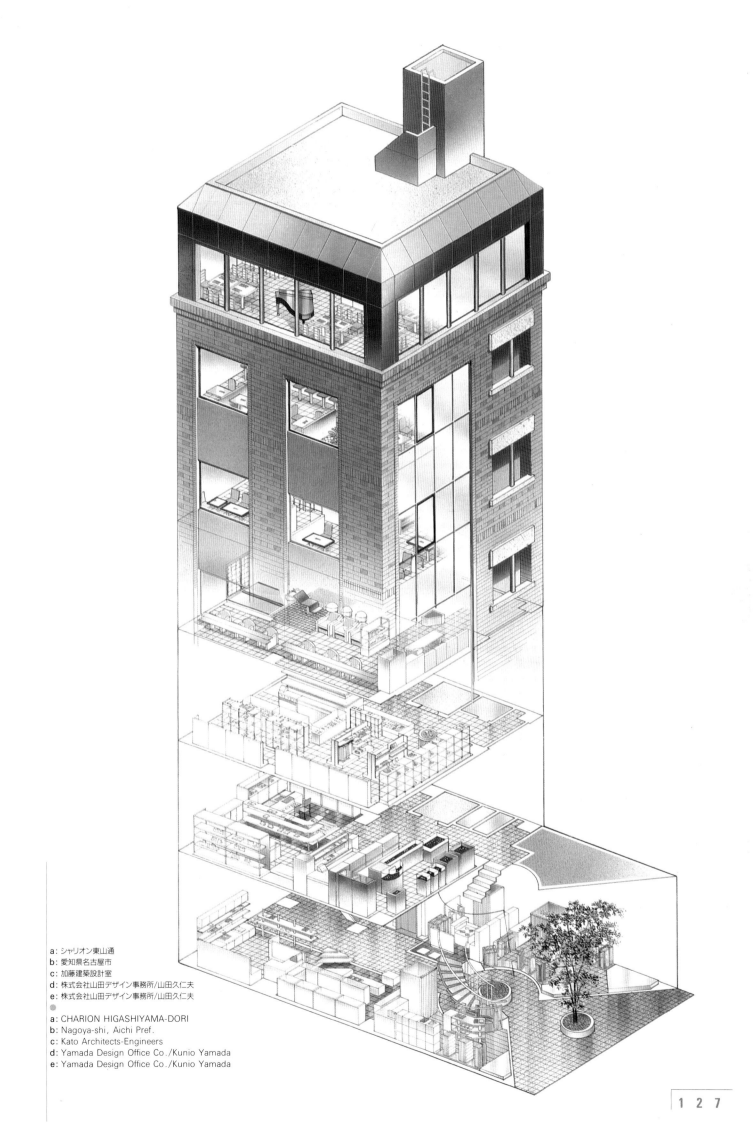

a: シャリオン東山通
b: 愛知県名古屋市
c: 加藤建築設計室
d: 株式会社山田デザイン事務所/山田久仁夫
e: 株式会社山田デザイン事務所/山田久仁夫

a: CHARION HIGASHIYAMA-DORI
b: Nagoya-shi, Aichi Pref.
c: Kato Architects-Engineers
d: Yamada Design Office Co./Kunio Yamada
e: Yamada Design Office Co./Kunio Yamada

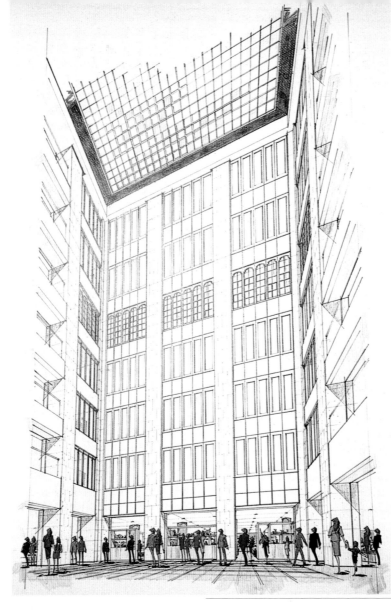

a: 銀座M
b: 東京都中央区銀座
c: 乃村工藝社
d: 柳川敏行
e: 柳川敏行

a: GINZA-M
b: Ginza, Chuo-ku, Tokyo
c: Nomura Co., Ltd.
d: Toshiyuki Yanagawa
e: Toshiyuki Yanagawa

a: インテリジェントビル
c: 株式会社電通/ハタスペース株式会社
d: ハタスペース株式会社
e: ハタスペース株式会社/秦昌八

a: INTERIJENT BUILDING
c: Dentsu Co., Ltd./Hata Space Co., Ltd.
d: Hata Space Co., Ltd.
e: Hata Space Co., Ltd./Shohachi Hata

a: コリンズ15 エントランス
b: 東京都新宿区歌舞伎町
c: 石原トータルプランニング株式会社
d: 柳田恵美子
e: アトリエShe

●
a: COLLINS 15-ENTRANCE
b: Kabuki-cho, Shinjuku-ku, Tokyo
c: Ishihara Total Planning Inc.
d: Emiko Yanagida
e: Atelier She

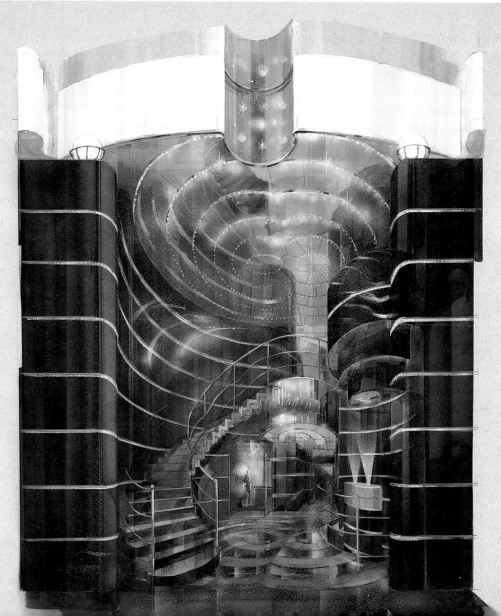

a: コリンズ六本木
b: 東京都港区六本木
c: 石原トータルプランニング株式会社
d: 柳田恵美子
e: アトリエShe

●
a: COLLINS ROPPONGI
b: Roppongi, Minato-ku, Tokyo
c: Ishihara Total Planning Inc.
d: Emiko Yanagida
e: Atelier She

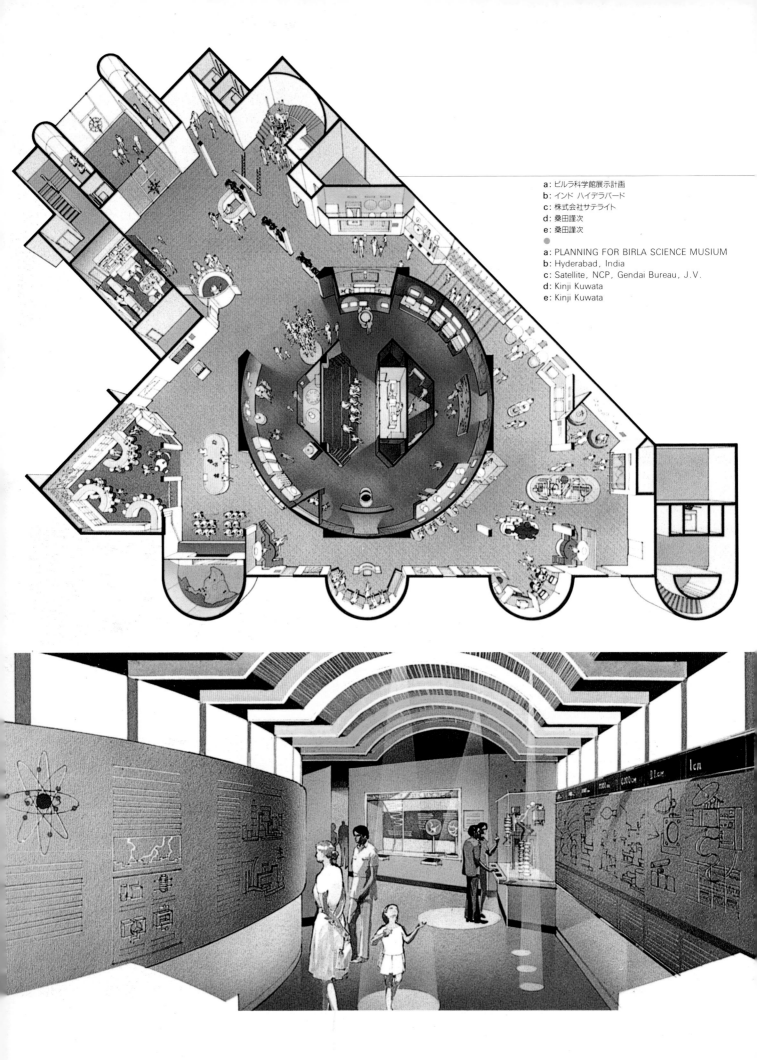

a: ビルラ科学館展示計画
b: インド ハイデラバード
c: 株式会社サテライト
d: 桑田謹次
e: 桑田謹次

●
a: PLANNING FOR BIRLA SCIENCE MUSIUM
b: Hyderabad, India
c: Satellite, NCP, Gendai Bureau, J.V.
d: Kinji Kuwata
e: Kinji Kuwata

a: ショールーム スタジオ　　a: NEC VIDEO STUDIO-SHOWROOM
b: 東京都千代田区　　　　　b: Chiyoda-ku, Tokyo
c: 日本電気デザインセンター　c: NEC Design Center
d: 桑田謹次　　　　　　　　d: Kinji Kuwata
e: 桑田謹次　　　　　　　　e: Kinji Kuwata

a: パソコン ショールーム
b: 東京都千代田区
c: 日本電気デザインセンター
d: 桑田謹次
e: 桑田謹次

a: NEC SHOWROOM
b: Chiyoda-ku, Tokyo
c: NEC Design Center
d: Kinji Kuwata
e: Kinji Kuwata

『夕景パースの効果的な描法』
坂井田將齊/優実

"The Effective Drawing Method of
Evening Perspectives"
by Masanari Sakaida & Yumi Sakaida

物件名❖スーパー・ライト
Project Title❖SUPER LIGHT

作画者❖坂井田將齊/坂井田優実
Renderer❖Masanari Sakaida & Yumi Sakaida

住所❖〒451 愛知県名古屋市西区新道1-17-18　エルファ アーキテクト
Address❖ELFA ARCHITECT 1-17-18, Shinmichi, Nishi-ku, Nagoya-shi,
Aichi Pref., 451　Tel.❖052-581-0976　Fax.❖052-581-0976

01 「エスキスを描く」通常は，レジャー系施設。インテリシェントビル，商業ビルの外観デザインなどの，建築パースを主に行っているが，今回のパースはデザインから入っている。まず，ラフスケッチを具体的に画面化して行く。

02 「コンピュータ入出力」図面を入力し，ベストアングル(距離・角度・アイレベル)を決める。コンピュータの利用で，R面や三次曲線，装飾の多い物件も正確かつ，短時間の入出力が可能になる。I.S.T社の「CATIST A3000」を使用。出力したものをラインパースとして仕上げ，エスキスと共に提出，打ち合わせで必要があれば修正。クライアントはこの段階で，本設計に入る。

03 「トレスダウン」設定したサイズのボードに対して，バランス良い大きさに拡大または縮小した下図を転写。今回は夕景パースのため，建物上部のモノレール状ダクトなど空と接する線は，ボード表面に溝が入る位の強さで写す。R面はあらゆるカーブ定規で，狂いのないよう慎重にはっきりとトレスダウンすること。キャンソンボード，イエローグレー・343を使用。

04 「トレスダウンに添景・車を描き加える」遠景は薄い線で，車は建物の妨げとならない場所にバランス良く配置。人物は着彩仕上の際に入れる。

05 「空を描く・その1」予め上空，中空，低空の色彩計画を立て，空の色を作っておく。空を塗る部分にハケで水を打つ。適度に馴んだところで色塗り開始。この時，画板が床と平行でないと絵具が流れてしまうので要注意。

06 「空を描く・その2」水分量に気をつけて絵具を溶く。太めの平筆にたっぷりと絵具を含ませ，一気に塗ってゆく。空の色は物件，ロケーションにより，その都度変えるが，今回は以下のとおり。上空＝プルシャンブルー，コバルトブルー，セピア。中空＝コバルトバイオレット，バントシエンナ，スカイブルー，コーラル。低空＝ブルーグレー，オレンジ，パーマネントイエロー，ホワイト。全てニッカー。

07 「空を描く・その3」グラデーションは前の色の付いた筆を洗わずに，軽く布で拭い，次の色を含ませる。細かな塗り残しに注意しながら，下空部まで大胆に下ろす。

08 「修正」空が乾ききらないうちに，建物に掛った絵具を手早くティッシュ等で，拭き取る。

09 「室内の表現・その1」前提として，昼間パースとは光の作用が逆になる事に留意して描くこと。まず調子を摑むため，薄い色から何度も重ね塗りしてゆく。絵具が乾かないのに次の色を重ねたり，度に濃く塗らないようにする。ここでは室内全体の流れだけを描く。絵具はイエロー(ペリカン・透明水彩)，インディアン・イエロー(ペリカン・透明水彩)，イエロー・オーカー(ホルベイン・透明水彩)，イエロー・グレイ(ホルベイン・透明水彩)，ウォーム・セピア(ウィンザー&ニュートン・透明水彩)，ブルー・グレー(ニッカー)，ホワイト(ターナー)，などを使用。

10 「室内の表現・その2」大まかな奥行きをつけてゆく。前ホール垂壁，遊戯台の並びを捕らえる。明るさの中にもコントラストをはっきりつける事が，ポイントになる。

事務所風景。 A view of the office.

スタッフ(左から)
坂井田將齊(MASANARI SAKAIDA)。
坂井田優実(YUMI SAKAIDA)。
加藤晴美(HARUMI KATOH)。
熊崎達彦(TATSUHIKO KUMAZAKI)。
Staff members (from left to right)
Masanori Sakaida, Yumi Sakaida,
Harumi Kato, Tatsuhiko Kumazaki.

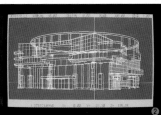

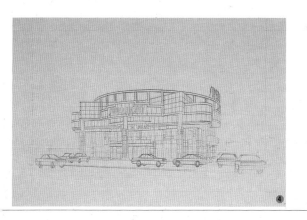

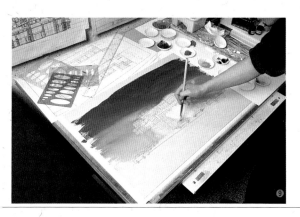

01 Drawing esquisse. Under usual conditions we use architectural perspective plans for work on such places as leisure facilities, inteligent buildings and the exterior design of commercial buildings, but in this case we will use the perspective design. Initially a rough sketch is made which will then be developed into the concrete drawing.

02 Computer input and output. Data is input into the computer to decide angles (distance angles and eye-levels). By using a computer a great deal of accuracy can be achieved in a short amount of time for works that have many rounded angles, 3-dimensional curves and decorations. In this case an I.S.T.CATIST A3000 is used. The completed work is output as a line prespective drawing and esquisse. The necessary amendments should be made during the arrangements. It is at this stage that the client begins the actual design work.

03 Trace down. Transfer the rough sketch that has been evenly enlarged or scaled down to fit the fixed size of the board. As this perspective drawing is set in the evening, the lines which adjoin the sky, such as the monorail ducts above the building, should be traced strongly enough to leave grooves on the board. The curved lines should be traced precisely with the use of all available curvilinear rulers. A Canson board and yellow-grey 343 is used.

04 Drawing an additional view and cars on the top of the trace down. Long distance views should be drawn lightly and the cars must be placed in positions that do not interfere with the balance of the drawing. The people should be drawn in at the coloring stage.

05 Drawing the sky (No. 1). The colors for the top, middle area and bottom of the sky should be decided beforehand. A layer of water should then be brushed onto the section earmarked as the sky. Once a moderate layer has been placed, the coloring will commence. It is necessary from time-to-time to place the board in a horizontal position to prevent the paint from running.

06 Drawing the sky (No. 2). Taking care of the amount of water used, thin down the paint. Load a flat brush with paint and spread the available volume over the paper. The colors used for the sky depends on the work and location, but in this case the following have been used. Top sky: Prusian blue, cobalt blue, sepia. Mid sky: Cobalt violet, burnt sienna, sky blue. Low sky: Blue-grey, orange, permanent yellow, white.

07 Drawing the sky (No. 3). Instead of washing the brush after each color, wipe it lightly with a cloth and then load it with the next color. This will enhance the effect of graduation. Work the brush from the top to the bottom very carefully in order not to leave any gaps.

08 Alteration. Any paint splashed on the buildings should be wiped off quickly with a tissue before it has time to dry.

09 Expression of the interior rooms (No. 1). Ensure that the light works opposite to day-time perspectives. To begin with, a light color should be painted on in several coats until the correct value of the color is reached. Be careful not to paint over wet paint or to paint in the darker colors in one go. At this stage only the folw of the room interiors is painted. The colors used here are; Yellow (P), Indian yellow (P), yellow ochre (H), yellow-grey (H), warm sepia (W), blue-grey (N), and white (T).

10 Expression of the interior rooms (No. 2). Add the rough depth. It is important to get the vertical wall of the front hall and the rows of strips just right. Make sure that the contrast is marked clearly even with the lighter colors.

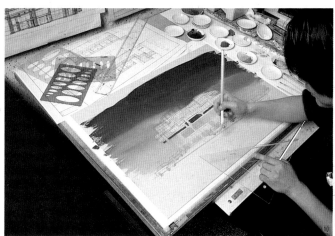

11 「室内・細部を描き込む」室内においての質感を表現する。照明関係，ハイライトを付ける。大判ガラスは，室内装飾品等のスポイルした質感による表現されるので，単色を用いないよう注意が必要。ガラスの重なる部分，リブは室内と同系色の影色で描く。

12 「室内仕上り」一応，外部ではあっても室内に掛かる部分の柱は，この段階で描いておくこと。夜間においてのステンレスは，闇を拾う部分と光を拾う部分が，極端なのが特徴。

13 「室内仕上り」

14 「空・室内のエアブラシ」空，室内で使用したものと同色の絵具を用いる。筆描きの時より多めの水で溶き，吹き付ける。現段階では，マスキングフイルムは不用。筆描きで不足した空の表現を，仕上った室内のイメージから調整してゆく。同時に，ボードの切れ端を利用した簡単なマスキングで，遠景を加える。絵具はウォーム・セピア（ウインザー＆ニュートン・透明水彩），イエロー・グレイ（ホルベイン・透明水彩），プルシャン・ブルー（ホルベイン・透明水彩）。室内の照明表現にエアブラシは効果的だが，かけすぎに気をつけたい。また，色を変える都度にノズルを洗うことを忘れずに。使用ハンドピースはオリンポス 101。

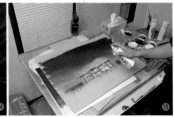

15 「定着液をかける」エアブラシ作業を終えたら，トリパブ A をかけておく。これは，以降の作業中にエアブラシ面が，擦れるのを防ぐため。トリパブの近距離からの吹き付けは，画面にシミを作る危険があるので要注意。

16 「空・室内エアブラシ後」

17 「外壁を塗る・その 1」空で作り上げたイメージを守り，周囲の環境が，どのように影響し，映り，変化してゆくかを把握する。仕様の質感を損なわぬよう配慮したい。しかし，商業建築物である以上，この上に活気と「艶」を持たせるため，多少，誇張した感覚的表現が必要となる。手前の柱にはブラケットが付くので，予め，光の映り込みをつけておく。絵の具はニッカーのブルー・グレー，イエロー・オーカー，スカイ・ブルー，セルリアン・ブルー，コバルト・ブルー，コバルト・バイオレット，バント・シエンナ，コーラル，それに，ホワイト（ターナー・ガッシュ），ウォーム・セピア（ウインザー＆ニュートン・透明水彩），イエロー・グレイ（ホルベイン・透明水彩），プルシャン・ブルー（ホルベイン・透明水彩）を使用。

18 「外壁を塗る・その 2」市松模様（カラーガラスとミラーガラスの貼分け）の表現は，視点からの距離，角度における明度の変化を考え，グリッド単位のグラデーションを作る。大庇（ホーロー鋼板）と共にエアブラシで，ハレーションをつけ，質感を補う。

19 「外壁・エアブラシ前」

20 「外壁・エアブラシ後」

21 「目地・ダクトの表現」市松，大庇の目地を入れてゆく。ここでも距離感をつけるため，手前の目地は濃くはっきりと，遠くの目地は細かく薄く引く。大庇ダクト（ステンレス鏡面仕上）は，後のネオン管類を目立たせるため，闇色で。同様に，上部ダクト（ホーロー鋼板）も濃く描いておく。

22 「目地・ダクト」

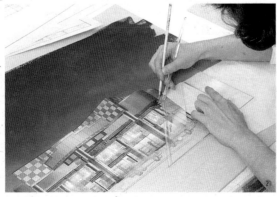

11 Brushing in the detail for the interior rooms. The quality featured in the rooms should be expressed. Add the Nebrabox (neon), the lighting and highlights. Be sure not to use a single color for the larger panes of glass as the interior decorations should be expressed on the windows. The ribs where the panes overlap should be painted in the same shadowy hues that was used for the room interiors.

12 The completion of the interiors. Although they are part of the external work, the pillars built over the windows should be painted in at this stage. It is one of the distinguishing features of stainless steel that the dark colors and light colors are picked out in extreme contrast.

13 The room interiors completed.

14 Airbrushing the sky and rooms. The same colors that were used for the sky and the interiors should be used. These colors should be thinned down with more water than was used for the brush work and then airbrushed on. It is not necessary to use masking tape at this point. Coordinate the sky that cuold not be expressed by the plain brush by comparing the image of the completed room interiors. At the same time, put in the long-distance view by using a board as a simple mask. The paints used here are; warm sepia (W) yellow-grey (H), and Prussian blue (H). The airbrush is effective for expressing the lighting within the rooms, but care should be taken not to spray on too much. The airbrush nozzles must be cleaned after each color. The handpiece used here is the Olympus 101.

15 Spray on the fixing solution. Spray the Tripab fixant onto the areas where the airbrushing is finished. This will prevent the airbrushed surface from becoming rubbed during the following proceedures. The fixant should not be sprayed on too close to the surface as this will leave marks.

16 The sky and interior after the airbrushing is completed.

17 Painting the exterior walls (No.1). A good grasp of the surroundings should be made with special attention given to the effect of reflection to ensure that the image of the completed sky is not altered. Although the quality should not be tampered with, with commercaial buildings it is necessary to add a little sensuous exageration to give a bright and lively surface impression. As a bracket needs to be added on the pillar in the foreground, the reflection of the light should be drawn in beforehand. The paints used here are; blue-grey, yellow ochre, sky-blue, cerulean blue, cabalt blue, cobalt violet, burnt sienna (N), white (T), warm sepia (W), yellow-gery (H), and Prussian blue (H).

18 Painting the exterior walls (No.2). Create the graduation in grid-form while concentrating on the distance available from the visual point and the change of the brightness due to the angles in order to express the check patterns (painted with New San Pitro blue and criamea). Supply the texture along the eaves (bonded steel sheets) with the use of an airbrush.

19 Exteriro walls before spraying with the airbrush.

20 Exterior walls after spraying with the airbrush.

21 The expression of the grain and ducts. Add the grain to the check pattern and the the large eaves. To express the feeling of distance as apparent in the picture, the foreground grain should be painted dark and clearly, while the grain for the distant parts should be light and vague. The large eave duct (with a stainless steel mirror finish) should be painted in dark colors to make the neon in the background prominent. The top duct (bonded stainless steel) should be painted even darker.

22 The grain and ducts.

23 「側面を塗る」上部ダクト支柱は円に沿っているので，側面も向きによって明度に変化をつけるが，ダクト上裏との差も，付けなければならない。正面性が強いアングルの絵の側面は，奥行が詰まっているので，グラデーションを強く，目地引にも差をつける。狭い面積の部分はコントラストをはっきり表わすこと。

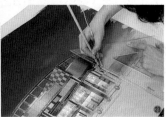

24 「側面仕上り」

25 「遠景を描く」今回は郊外の店舗で，周辺が駐車場になっているため，近距離の建築物は無い。遠景は，特に深みを出す役割を持つ。夕景に溶け込むよう彩度を落とし，弱く描き，足もとを締めるように心掛けよう。

26 「電飾関係を描く・その１」レジャー系施設の特徴として，電飾が非常に多い事が掲げられるが，一般の設計図とは別途に，電飾業者が設計した「ネオン図」がある。電飾を軽く描いてしまうと，絵全体が台無しになるので，相当に注意を払う必要がある。スコッチカル（外装用カッティングシート）の指定により，絵具に蛍光色を混ぜる場合もあるが，蛍光色の入れ過ぎは後に変色の原因となってしまう。

27 「電飾関係を描く・その２」ネオン類はトランスにより，光が流れたり点滅しているが，絵では全て点燈した状態を描く。Ｒ面のネオン管は，非常に目立つので慎重に描くこと。

28 「上部ダクト・側面チャンネル」

29 「電飾関係を描く・その３」側面に付くネオンも夜間においては，あえて明度を落とす必要はない。柱のとりまき，ダウンライト等も付け，これで一応，建物の部分は完成。使用絵具はブリリアント・レッド（ターナー），ピンク（ターナー），蛍光ルミ・スカーレット（ニッカー），コバルト・グリーン（ニッカー），セルリアン・ブルー（ニッカー），プルシャン・ブルー（ニッカー），クローム・イエロー（ニッカー），ホワイト（ターナー）。

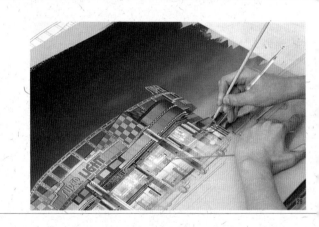

30 「建物仕上り・添景へ」

31 「添景を描く・その１」路面をぬる時に車の下書きが隠れてしまうので，車の位置を確認する意味で自動車ガラスを描いておく。建物からの光の映り方に気を配ろう。

32 「添景を描く・その２」路面を表現する。室内からの光，反射を把握した上で大胆に描くこと。実際より反射を強調させ，深い色で足元を引締め，建物の存在感を出す。

33 「添景を描く・その３」柱の映り込みを表わす。添景にも動きを持たせるため，縦横のシャープな筆運びが必要。道路境界線なども描き込む。絵具はシルバー・グレー（ターナー），ライト・グリーン（ターナー），ホワイト（ターナー），バント・シエンナ（ニッカー），セピア（ニッカー），コバルト・バイオレット（ニッカー），イエロー・オーカー（ニッカー），ブルー・グレー（ニッカー），オレンジ（ニッカー），イエロー・グレイ（ホルベイン・透明水彩），プルシャン・ブルー（ホルベイン・透明水彩），ウォーム・セピア（ニュートン・透明水彩）を使用。

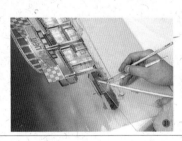

34 「添景・車を描く」車は建物のスケール感を表したり，動きのある物として，絵を活気立たせる役割りを持っている。建物を最も効果的に見せる配色を選ぶこと。金属的かつ暖かみのある表現で，やや小振りに描く。

35 「車仕上り」

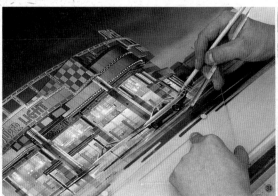

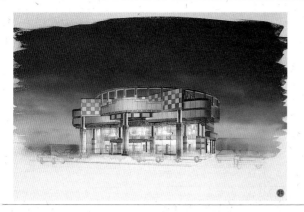

23 Painting the sides. As the top duct follows a circle, the change should be added to the value of the colors of the sides. The difference apparent at the back of the top duct must be distinguised. The graduation on the sides of the building should be drawn boldly as the depth is blocked. The lines of the grain should also be discriminated. Express clearly the contrast on the narrow areas.

24 The sides finished.

25 Drawing the distant view. As the shops are located in the suburbs and the area surrounding the building is car-park, there are no buildings in the immediate vicinity. The long distance view will provide the finished picture with depth. Paint it very lightly with dark colors so it merges into the evening scene. The lines nearer the bottom should be emphasized.

26 Adding the illuminations (No.1). As one of the distinguishing characters of the leisure facility is neon illuminations, it is necessary to becom involved with the neon chart in addition to the general drawing. Much attention must be paid to the illuminations as failure to do so will destroy the overall effect of the picture. It is possible to mix flourescent coloring with the paint, but this must not be overdone as it will cause later fading.

27 Adding the illuminations (No.2). Although neon lights flash on and off, in the picture they are drawn as if all are on. The round strip-lighting should be drawn on carefully as it stands out in the picture.

28 The top duct and side channel.

29 Adding the illuminations (No.3). It is not necessary to use lighter colors for the neon lighting on the side of the building at night. Having drawn the surrounding pillar ornaments and downlights, the work on the building is finished. The paints used here are; brilliant red (T), pink (T), lumi scarlet (N), cobalt green (N), cerulean blue (N), Prussian blue (N), chrome yellow (N) and white (T).

30 The building is completed. The next step is the detached view.

31 Drawing the detached view (No.1). As the rough sketches of the cars are painted in when the road surface is added, the glass of the car windows must be painted in to confirm their positions. Pay attention to the angle of light reflected from the building.

32 Drawing the detached views (No.2). Express the road surface. Draw it in boldly after considering the light and reflection that pierces from the rooms. Deep colors need to be used to form the base of the picture in order to produce the effective existance of the building.

33 Drawing the detached views (No.3). Express the reflection of the pillar. Up and down movements of a sharp brush are needed to add movement to the detatched view. Draw in the border-line of the road as well. The paints used here are; silver-grey (T), light-green (T), white (T), burnt sienna (N), sepia (N), cobalt violet (N), yellow ochre (N), blue-grey (N), orange (N), yellow-grey (H), Prussian blue (H), and warm sepia (N).

34 Drawing the detached view. Cars play the role of indicating the scale of the building and provide a liveliness to the picture as they are moving objects. The most effective colors in contrast to the building should be chosen for the cars. They should be drawn slightly smaller with a metallic effect, but with a warmth inside.

35 The completion of the cars.

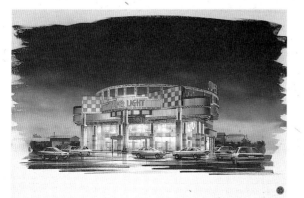

36 「エアブラシで仕上げる」柱ブラケット，サーチライト，車のヘッドライトなど，ボードの切端を利用したマスキングで吹いてゆく。白熱球類の光りは，白に微量の黄を混ぜたものを用いる。

37 「チェック」これまでの最終的なチェック。描き落としが無いかどうか調べたり，修正を行う。

38 「人物を描く」人物は車や人物どうしと重ねる事により，絵の奥行きを出す。雰囲気や動きを表現するため，アドリブ的に描いてゆく。この場合，逆光なので彩度を落とす。

39 「添景・人物上り」

40 「完成」

36 Complete the picture with the use of the airbrush. Spray on the pillar brackets, the search lights and headlights of the cars with the aid of a piece of card board as masking. The beams of light are painted in white with a touch of yellow.

37 Checking. The final check should include an overall scrutiny to ensure nothing has been left out. It is at this time that the alterations are also made.

38 Drawing the people. The depth of the picture is produced by the overlaying people. Draw then in an ad-lib style to express the atmosphere and movemnet. The degree of coloring should be dropped slightly if the people are featured before light.

39 The completion of the detatched view and the people.

40 Completion

5.索引

建築物名称　　Project Title

設 計 事 務 所　　Planning Office

作 画 者　Renderer

出 品 者 / Applicant

応 募 代 表 者　Representative of Applicant

赤坂孝史
神奈川県横浜市港北区日吉本町1-23-12ライオンズ日吉台302 〒223,
アカサカレンダリング　Tel.044-62-9477

安土実
東京都渋谷区本町6-2-21メゾンヒロ201 〒151,アヅチ・プランニングスタジオ
Tel.03-378-6126

アトリエボノム
東京都渋谷区千駄ケ谷4-9-24メゾンドール北参道319 〒151,
有限会社アトリエボノム　Tel.03-405-5852

株式会社イシダ建築デザイン・デザイン部
京都府京都市南区上鳥羽塔ノ森東向町84-1 〒601,株式会社イシダ建築デザイン
Tel.075-671-6150

伊東剛
北海道上富良野町深山峠あほの村 〒071-04,A.H.O.pro
Tel.0167-45-4487

井内一夫
兵庫県西宮市川添町14-12 〒662,有限会社スタジオゼロ
Tel.0798-36-0287

大石敏雄
東京都豊島区東池袋3-8-5パレドール池袋202 〒170,敏デザイン事務所
Tel.03-983-6264

大山記糸夫
東京都新宿区冨久町2-19市ケ谷ヒルサイドハイツ202 〒162
Tel.03-359-4593

奥村一也
東京都渋谷区神宮前2-4-20外苑アスペイア1F 〒150,
有限会社ヒューマン・ファクター　Tel.03-402-2683

小倉通子
東京都世田谷区尾山台1-10-9 〒158,有限会社スタジオ・オーブル
Tel.03-704-5307

株式会社オズ・アトリエ
東京都港区南青山2-5-9パールビル南青山 〒107,株式会社オズ・アトリエ
Tel.03-408-4766

小野垣晋一
東京都渋谷区神宮前2-4-20外苑アスペイア1F 〒150,
有限会社ヒューマン・ファクター　Tel.03-402-2683

海法一夫
東京都渋谷区笹塚3-2-3ベルプラザ401 〒151,有限会社海法デザイン事務所
Tel.03-374-2455

笠原征人
神奈川県横浜市中区本牧原5-1-508 〒231
Tel.045-622-3116

鹿島建設株式会社
東京都港区赤坂6-5-30 〒107
Tel.03-5561-2111

加藤春枝
東京都三鷹市中原1-7-28-310 〒181,ケイズ
Tel.03-307-0416

金本正
香川県高松市藤塚町3-4-6 〒760,有限会社金本デザイン事務所
Tel.0878-34-1765

川嶋俊介
愛媛県伊予郡松前町北黒田520-2 〒791-31,川嶋レンダリングオフィス有限会社
Tel.0899-84-8498

川原崎由夫
大阪府大阪市北区松ヶ枝町6-17第7新興ビル803 〒530,スタジオ・アーク
Tel.06-352-8890

桑田謹次
東京都目黒区平町1-20-17-102 〒152,株式会社アトリエ
Tel.03-724-2382

近藤喬枝
神奈川県横浜市緑区美しが丘4-32-23 〒227
Tel.044-901-6811

斉藤富子
東京都練馬区中村南1-30-15 〒176,とみあとりえ
Tel.03-998-7349

坂井田將齊
愛知県名古屋市西区新道1-17-18 〒451,エルファ アーキテクト
Tel.052-581-0976

坂井田優実
愛知県名古屋市西区新道1-17-18 〒451,エルファ アーキテクト
Tel.052-581-0976

四海隼一
兵庫県姫路市勝原区山戸22 〒671-12,隼デザイン事務所
Tel.0792-73-6616

庄司澄子
宮城県仙台市清水沼1-1-12 〒983,株式会社潤建築工房
Tel.022-293-4502

進士竜一
東京都文京区本駒込5-67-1クレール駒込511 〒113
Tel.03-943-8345

諏訪利弘
群馬県前橋市南町2-18-15 〒371,スワデザイン
Tel.0272-23-3855

高野浩毅
東京都千代田区内神田1-7-11竜ビル3F 〒101,インテリア・ライフ101
Tel.03-293-9249

譚少芝
千葉県船橋市行田3-2-16-410 〒273
Tel.0474-39-7243

長尾恵美子
千葉県松戸市新松戸7-373 〒270,パース・スタヂオ
Tel.0473-45-0879

長谷川久彦
新潟県新潟市水道町2-5932-455 〒951,アトリエハセガワ

Tel.025-228-4600

秦舜八
大阪府大阪市東住吉区湯里2-19-16 〒546,ハタスペース株式会社
Tel.06-702-0389

古橋孝之
静岡県浜松市田町224-23 〒430,株式会社矢内店舗設計事務所
Tel.0534-54-8416

松村範也
大阪府大阪市中央区西心斎橋1-13-5サンダー心斎橋ビル10F 〒542,
株式会社レンダリングウルフ　Tel.06-243-3717

宮後浩
大阪府大阪市中央区南船場4-13-15コラムビル 〒542,
株式会社コラム・デザインセンター　Tel.06-245-4631

村山善次郎
千葉県習志野市谷津5-28-12 〒275,村山デザインスタジオ
Tel.0474-75-4355

柳川敏行
東京都町田市南大谷838-32 〒194,C.D.W.ジパング
Tel.0427-28-7766

柳田恵美子
東京都港区南青山6-1-6パレス青山207 〒107,アトリエShe
Tel.03-400-0371

山田久仁夫
愛知県名古屋市昭和区南山町9-1 〒466,株式会社山田デザイン事務所
Tel.052-833-9880

芳野明
大阪府大阪市淀川区西中島4-8-20-102 〒532,よしのデザイン事務所
Tel.06-303-5448

吉村勲
和歌山県和歌山市和歌山浦西1-4-51セジュール雑賀203号 〒641,
建築パース・アトリエ・ノバ　Tel.0734-45-5871

和田宅矛
静岡県浜松市野口町218-1 〒430,造研
Tel.0534-63-7637

Akira Yoshino
Yoshino Desing Offiec,4-8-20-102,Nishi-Nakajima,Yodogawa-ku,Osaka-shi,Osaka,532
Tel.06-303-5448

Atelier Bonhomme
Atelier Bonhomme Ltd.,319,Maison Doll Kita-sando,4-9-24,Sendagaya,Shibuya-ku,Tokyo,151
Tel.03-405-5852

Emiko Nagao
Pers Studio,7-373,Shin-Matsudo,Matsudo-shi,Chiba Pref.,270
Tel.0473-45-0879

Emiko Yanagida
Atelier She,207,Palace Aoyama,6-1-6,Minami-Aoyama,Minato-ku,Tokyo,107
Tel.03-400-0371

Go Ito
A.H.O.pro,Ahono-mura,Miyama-toge,Kami-Furano-cho,Hokkaido,071-04
Tel.0167-45-4487

Harue Kato
Keiz,1-7-28-310,Nakahara,Mitaka-shi,Tokyo,181
Tel.03-307-0416

Hiroki Takano
Interior Life 101,Ryu Building 3F,1-7-11,Uchi-Kanda,Chiyoda-ku,Tokyo,101
Tel.03-293-9249

Hiroshi Miyago
Column Design Center Inc.,Column Building,4-13-15,Minami-Senba,Chuo-ku,Osaka-shi,Osaka,542
Tel.06-245-4631

Hisahiko Hasegawa
Atelier Hasegawa,2-5932-455,Suido-cho,Niigata-shi,Niigata Pref.,951
Tel.025-228-4600

Isao Yoshimura
Kenchiku Pers Atelier NOVA,203,Sejour Saika,1-4-51,Wakayama-Uranishi,Wakayama-shi,Wakayama Pref.,641
Tel.0734-45-5871

Ishida Architectural Design Office Co.,Design Section
Ishida Architectural Design Office Co.,84-1,Higashi-Mukai-machi,Tonomori,Kami-Toba,Minami-ku,Kyoto-shi,Kyoto,601
Tel.075-671-6150

Itsuo Kaiho
Design Room Kaihoh Inc.,401,Belle Plaza,3-2-3,Sasazuka,Shibuya-ku,Tokyo,151
Tel.03-374-2455

Kajima Corporation
6-5-30,Akasaka,Minato-ku,Tokyo,107
Tel.03-5561-2111

Kazaya Okumura
Human Factor Ltd.,Gaien Aspeia 1F,2-4-20,Jingumae,Shibuya-ku,Tokyo,150
Tel.03-402-2683

Kazuo Inouchi
Studio Zero,14-12,Kawazoe-cho,Nishinomiya-shi,Hyogo Pref.,662
Tel.0798-36-0287

Kinji Kuwata
ATELIER Co.,1-20-17-102,Taira-machi,Meguro-ku,Tokyo,152
Tel.03-724-2382

Kishio Oyama
202,Ichigaya Hill Side Heights,2-19,Tomihisa-cho,Shinjuku-ku,Tokyo,162
Tel.03-359-4593

Kunio Yamada
Yamada Design Office Co.,9-1,Nanazan-cho,Showa-ku,Nagoya-shi,Aichi Pref.,446
Tel.052-833-9880

Masanari Sakaida
ELFA ARCHITECT 1-17-18,Shinmichi,Nishi-ku,Nagoya-shi,Aichi Pref.,451
Tel.052-581-0976

Masato Kasahara
5-1-508,Honmokuhara,Naka-ku,Yokohama-shi,Kanagawa Pref.,231
Tel.045-622-3116

Michiko Ogura
Studio Oburu,1-10-9,Oyamadai,Setagaya-ku,Tokyo,158
Tel.03-704-5307

Minoru Azuchi
Azuchi Planning Studio,201,Mezon Hiro,6-2-21,Hon-cho,Shibuya-ku,Tokyo,151
Tel.03-378-6126

Noriya Matsumura
Rendering WOLF Co.,Ltd.,Thunder Shinsaibashi Building 10F,1-13-5,Nishi-Shinsaibashi,Chuo-ku,Osaka-shi,Osaka,542
Tel.06-243-3717

OZ-Atelier Co.,Ltd.
OZ-Atelier Co.,Ltd.,Pearl Building Minami-Aoyama,2-5-9,Minami-Aoyama,Minato-ku,Tokyo,107
Tel.03-408-4766

Ryuichi Shinji
511,Clair-Komagome,5-67-1,Honkomagome,Bunkyo-ku,Tokyo,113
Tel.03-943-8345

Shinichi Onogaki
Human Facter Ltd.,Gaien Aspeia 1F,2-4-20,Jingumae,Shibuya-ku,Tokyo,150
Tel.03-402-2683

Shohachi Hata
Hata Space Co.,Ltd.,2-19-16,Yuzato,Higashi-Sumiyoshi-ku,Osaka-shi,Osaka,546
Tel.06-702-0389

Shunichi Shikai
Hayabusa Design Office,22,Yamato,Katsuhara-ku,Himeji-shi,Hyogo Pref.,671-12
Tel.0792-73-6616

Shunsuke Kawashima
Kawashima Rendering Office,520-2,Kita-Kuroda,Masaki-cho,Iyo-gun,Ehime Pref.,791-31
Tel.0899-84-8498

Sumiko Shoji
JUN Architectural Design Office,1-1-12,Shimizunuma,Sendai-shi,Miyagi Pref.,983
Tel.022-293-4502

Tadashi Kanemoto
Kanemoto Desing Office,3-4-6,Fujitsuka-cho,Takamatsu-shi,Kagawa Pref.,760
Tel.0878-34-1765

Takae Kondo
4-32-23,Utsukushigaoka,Midori-ku,Yokohama-shi,Kanagawa Pref.,227
Tel.044-901-6811

Takashi Akasaka
Akasaka Rendering,302,Laions Hiyoshidai,1-23-12,Hiyoshi-Honcho,Kohoku-ku,Yokohama-shi,Kanagawa Pref.,223
Tel.044-62-9477

Takayuki Furuhashi
Yanai Design Office Co.,Ltd.,224-23,Tamachi,Hamamatsu-shi,Shizuoka Pref.,430
Tel.0534-54-8416

Takumu Wada
Zoken,218-1,Noguchi-cho,Hamamatsu-shi,Shizuoka Pref.,430
Tel.0534-63-7637

Tan Shao Zhi
3-2-16-410,Gyota,Funabashi-shi,Chiba Pref.,273
Tel.0474-39-7243

Tomiko Saito
Tomi Atelier,1-30-15,Nakamura-Minami,Nerima-ku,Tokyo,176
Tel.03-998-7349

Toshihiro Suwa
Suwa Design,2-18-15,Minami-cho,Maebashi-shi,Gunma Pref.,371
Tel.0272-23-3855

Toshio Oishi
Toshi Design Office,202,Paredool Ikebukuro,3-8-5,Higashi-Ikebukuro,Toshima-ku,Tokyo,170
Tel.03-983-6264

Toshiyuki Yanagawa
C.D.W.JIPANG,838-32,Minami-Oya,Machida-shi,Tokyo,194
Tel.0427-28-7766

Yoshio Kawarasaki
Studio Ark,803,Dai-nana Shinko Building,6-17,Matsugae-cho,Kita-ku,Osaka-shi,Osaka,530
Tel.06-352-8890

Yumi Sakaida
ELFA ARCHITECT 1-17-18,Shinmichi,Nishi-ku,Nagoya-shi,Aichi Pref.,451
Tel.052-581-0976

Zenjiro Murayama
Murayama Design Studio,5-28-12,Yatsu,Narashino-shi,Chiba Pref.,275
Tel.0474-75-4355

あ　と　が　き

　本来は，建築業界を中心に，設計図書の一部として，あるいは宣伝広告のために描かれ，扱われてきたパースが，作品集として世に出ることは，実に意義深いことである。

建築の企画，設計の各段階で描かれるパースは，各々の目的により，様々な表現要素を求められるが，基本的には，デザイン意図をいかに忠実に表現するかということである。建築空間を描くうえで，第一のポイントは，建築自体が未来を見据えたデザインワークであるために，レンダラーは設計者の（素材・デザインなどすべてに渡る）未来意識を，どこまで把握できるかにある，また建物あるいは室内空間の臨場感，演出効果のための環境をいかに描くかが，レンダラーに次に問われる資質ということになるだろうか。それらが的確に表現されて，パースは，合目的的情報資料としての役割を，より果しうることにもなる。すなわちパースは，それ自体が目的作品ではないにもかかわらず，単に設計図の二次的著作物ではなく，レンダラーの力量によって，その完成度が左右される一つの美術作品となる。そして，それらのパースは，建築がそうであるように，常に時代を反映し，未来を予見させる情報絵画としての生命をも持つ事にもなる。それが，今日パースが，建築以外の分野でも，読んで面白い絵，として着目され始めてきた所以であろうか。

　この度の企画，常に時代の先端的であり，洗練されている事を要求される，ショップ&レストランというテーマは，実は15年ぶりの登場である，先の作品集と比べてみるとき，正にパースが時代の証人である事を思い知らされる。改めて，本書を企画し，製作に奮闘された，大田氏の慧眼と，併せて，20年もの昔にパースの作品集出版に先鞭をつけられたグラフィック社の先見性に脱帽し，深く感謝するものであります。

　本書が建築，デザイン，美術を愛する多くの方々に，楽しく読んでいただける事を願って，あとがきとします。

　なお，本書は，ショップ&レストラン外装篇と一対をなすものとして企画されたパース作品集であり，本文中に収録されたパース製作プロセスは両書のまとめの意味で，坂井田氏による外観パースと進士氏による室内パースとを併載したものです。

大平善生

Originally prespective drawings were looked upon as design drawings or propaganda advertisements mainly for the architectural world, so it is of deep significance that they have finally made their presence felt in the eyes of the public as a collective work. Various expressive elements are demanded in each stage of the planning and design of perspective drawings, but basically the final effect will depend on how closely the actual idea of the design was expressed.

The most important point in the initial stages of drawing an architectual space is focused on how much the artist can grasp the awareness of the designers basic idea (through all areas including materials as well as design) as it is intented to express the actual finished article. The second point is focused on how the presence of the building, interior architecture and enviroment creation for the setting is solely dependent on the talents of the artist. It is very important that these are accurately expressed in order to promote the perspective drawing to accomplish its duty as a multipurpose piece of informative data. In other words, despite the fact that it is a non-purpose work, the perspective drawing itself could develop into only a secondary piece of designing, but an art work influenced by the abilities of the artist. Taken in this sense, prespective drawings will serve as informative paintings for the future as well as constant reflections of the age in the same way as the actual architecture. This could be one reason why perspective drawings are recently be taken seriously as interesting pictures which can be appreciated outside of the confines of architecture.

It has been fifteen years since the theme of shops and restaurants requiring the maintenance of constant trendidity and sophisticated elements ingenous to the era has been publicized. Comparing this collection to the previous one it becomes obvious that perspective drawing is acting as an actual witness of the times.

I would formally like to stand in bareheaded respect and indicate my deepest gratitude to the Graphic-sha Publishing Co., Ltd. who took the initiative to publish a collection of perspective drawing twenty years ago. It was under the merciful eye of Mr. Ota of the same company who put all of his efforts into the plans for the production of this book.

Hoping this publication will be enjoyed by many people who love arts, I draw to the end of this afterword.

Lastly, this book is a collection of perspective drawings designed to act a counterpart edition to "Shop and Restaurant Building Compilation of Exterior Pers Works". The combination of Mr. Sakaida's exterior and Mr. Shinji's interior have been used to serve the purpose of summing up the process of perspective productions from both books.

Zensei Ohira

Afterword

建築パース：内装
　―ショップ＆レストラン―

改訂第1刷発行　1994年8月25日

編　　集　グラフィック社
監　　修　日本アーキテクチュラル・レンダラーズ協会
装　　丁　箕浦 卓
レイアウト　箕浦 卓（デザイン協力：村田由樹子＋原 緑）

発 行 者　久世利郎
印　　刷　恒美印務有限公司
製　　本　恒美印務有限公司
写　　植　三和写真工芸株式会社

発　　行　株式会社グラフィック社
　　　　　〒102 東京都千代田区九段北1-9-12
　　　　　電話 03-3263-4318 / Fax.03-3263-5297

ISBN4-7661-0546-X